"This is the type of boo̲̲̲̲... y, but that is much need̲̲̲̲... it practice, written by a̲̲̲̲... it is clear, well-structure̲̲̲̲... e is that this book takes understanding of professional experience to a higher level. It dares to conceptualize coaching with an appreciation of complexity and lucid thinking, providing a coherent theoretical proposition built on new ideas and a meaningful synthesis of what the best of this field can currently offer. This book is great for both an intelligent novice and an advanced practitioner. I enjoyed reading it and cannot recommend it strongly enough."

Tatiana Bachkirova, Professor of Coaching
Psychology and Director of the International
Centre for Coaching and Mentoring Studies,
Oxford Brookes University, UK

"From the first few pages of this book, the authors capture the essence of the next evolutionary wave of coaching in organizations. It sparked my thinking immediately. Our clients, in their own words, are asking us as coaches and coaching practice leaders, to be more systemic in our approach. They want us to engage them and the complexity of the environment in which they lead. Coaching in Three Dimensions provided a comprehensive, yet elegant and straight forward, model as to how we can include the voice of clients, coaches and key organizational stakeholders. The model helped me reframe the strategic narrative for coaching in our organisation, in a way that has created clarity, shared meaning and accelerated decision making."

Karen R. Mathre, Coaching Center of
Excellence Leader, Medtronic

"The shift from linear to systemic thinking is fundamental to coach maturity – here is a book that lifts the lid on this complex but essential transition."

David Clutterbuck, Practice Leader,
David Clutterbuck Partnership

"This book is both refreshing and timely. Refreshing because it straightforwardly acknowledges the messiness of the coaching engagement, without offering simple solutions. Rather it honours the reader's intelligence by challenging us to think carefully and deeply about what we are doing, offering the promise of a richer, more enduring perspective. It's timely because this book is needed. Whilst everyone likes to talk about 'VUCA', few have been able to offer a coherent articulation of how coaches might within this complexity and chaos. This book offers precisely that."

Dr. Gordon Spence, Program Director, Master of
Business Coaching, Sydney Business School,
University of Wollongong

"As developmental needs in organizations have grown ever more complex, there is a need for coaches and coaching itself to evolve so they can rise to the occasion. The authors have laid out a clear path for doing so, particularly with their focus on systemic frames and the maturation of coaches. I highly recommend this book for raising the bar and casting light on the path ahead."

Dr. David Drake, Founder and CEO,
Moment Institute

"Many books about coaching only look at coaching as a tool but fail to take the world around us seriously into account. The authors start by recognizing the rapid changes taking place in the world and organizational life. Their inclusive and in-depth understanding of coaching, and developmental dialogue, will help the reader apply this work in service of renewing collaboration, organizational change and leadership."

Reinhard Stelter, Professor of Coaching
Psychology, University of Copenhagen

"Paul and Allen present a thoughtful and grounded treatment of coaching in 'real' organisations where quite often things don't make a lot of sense. They don't fall into the trap of debunking traditional approaches. Instead, they provide a model and weave a narrative that encourages multiple approaches. The underlying assumption is that complexity-of-context requires that coaches carry a complexity-of-mind. The writers draw on research, theory and experience to encourage coaches to embrace the systemic and messy nature of organisational life. There is an elegance in their approach that might well provide an attractor for coaches to step from the comfort of the familiar to the discomfort of the unknown – and enjoy the ride."

Geoff Abbott, Director Executive and
Organisational Coaching, Graduate
School of Business, Queensland
University of Technology

"The right coaching can offer profound value for individuals and organisations. A coaching culture is a real differentiator for companies and a must for the complexities we all need to face now and in the future of work. The tools and approaches in this book provide Human Resource professionals and OD practitioners with the toolkit to work effectively with executives, individuals and teams."

Raechel Gavin, Group Executive People &
Culture, Quantium

"Paul and Allen have produced a thoughtful book on coaching methods that draws together many strands of thought, research and practice across the coaching industry over the past 20 years. Their capacity to illustrate a range of approaches to coaching ensures that this book is an informative and interesting read that will speak to experienced coaches and managers."

Professor Michael Cavanagh, Deputy Director
Coaching Psychology Unit, School of Psychology,
the University of Sydney

"In *Coaching in Three Dimensions*, the authors take readers into coaching conversations, places we rarely have the opportunity to venture. The book challenges coaches to take their conversations to a deeper level, to truly understand the client's interests, beliefs and assumptions. Most helpful is the exploration of leaders in today's corporations, managing multiple systems and realities, their teams, and complex, matrixed organizations. The coach should consider all of these, not only the client as individual. This book should help even the most experienced coach co-create with clients more successfully. You won't want to put this book down!"

Alison Arkin, Global Manager of Learning and Development, Goodyear Tire and Rubber Company

"Although coaching receives plaudits across the board in talent development, it is plagued with unevenness in its delivery. Part of the problem is that many coaching approaches are prescriptive, and in their specificity they end up only adding to the overall confusion. Here, however, is a book in which the authors offer perspective rather than prescription. See how they merge approaches from the traditional, to the dialogic, to the systemic, and how they encourage coaches to work beyond the level of the individual. This is a contemporary book for coaches in the future organization – which has already arrived."

Joe Raelin, Knowles Chair, Northeastern University, Boston, USA

"This book is fantastic and can give you a new perspective on coaching. The authors look in depth at various approaches to coaching, including the increasingly popular but widely misunderstood 'leader as a coach'. Numerous real-life examples help even experienced coaches reflect on their own coaching style, and adjust for optimum outcomes. A gold mine not only for coaching practitioners, but any professional who wants to deepen their understanding of how coaching works."

Dr. Gerrit Pelzer, Leadership Advisor & Executive Coach, Bangkok

"If you read one book on coaching this year, let it be this book! Despite coaching's promise, traditional approaches too often fail to have the transformational impact clients and organizations crave. We need new thinking on how coaches can help clients keep pace with the demands a VUCA world places upon them. This book provides a breakthrough in thinking and will change how you think about your practice and the impact you can have with your clients and the world."

Laura Heaton, Vice President Talent
Development, Penske Truck Leasing

"The job of an organization is to bring multitudes of humans together, provide a shared purpose, and create something that is of value to customers. No easy task, humans are complicated. Our executives must learn, adjust and innovate to be successful. This book shows us that as coaches we are in the same boat. Knowing what's true today may not be true in a year. The authors challenge coaches to understand the system, and to work in much the same way as their clients, discovering and adapting to maximize results."

Rebecca Hemmer, Director of
Leadership Development, Edward Jones

"Many of us would love to be a fly on the wall and observe other people coaching. While that is rarely possible, *Coaching in Three Dimensions* offers a great alternative, with each chapter enriched with examples of coaching situations and dialogues. Drawing on a rich theoretical basis as well as extensive experience of coaching practice, the authors offer a highly readable text that invites the reader to reflect on their coaching practice and how they can develop their effectiveness as coaches in a highly complex, ambiguous and rapidly changing world. Well worth a read!"

Associate Professor Grace McCarthy,
Dean, Sydney Business School,
University of Wollongong

"Drawing on their considerable depth of experience, the authors reveal some astute insights and home truths of the coaching industry and the realities of coaching executives in a range of complex environments. The reader is provided a short-cut into the real world of organisational coaching; its positive impact and potential short-comings. Always insightful, sometimes irreverent to traditionalists, *Coaching in Three Dimensions* offers credible suggestions as to how coaches and coaching will need to adapt to the quickening and changing organisational landscape."

Tony Mathers, Chief Executive, Institute of
Executive Coaching and Leadership

Coaching in Three Dimensions

Traditional approaches to coaching fail to account for the way organisations really work. Attempts to enhance leadership capability one person at a time, through private one-to-one coaching sessions, are unlikely to succeed by themselves. *Coaching in Three Dimensions: Meeting the Challenges of a Complex World* offers a more connected, systemic approach, aligning coaching with the realities and challenges of organisations operating in an ever more complex world.

Coaching in Three Dimensions is structured around a central model: the three dimensions of coaching. Using stories and case studies, the book enables readers to:

1   Consider their current and desired *approach* to coaching: is it traditional, dialogic, or systemic?
2   Identify which areas of *practice* they work in and wish to work in: one-to-one coaching, group/team coaching, and/or organisational coaching?
3   Think about stretching their *development* as a coach in terms of competence, capability and perspective: how do you enhance your capacity to manage the challenges of increasing complexity?

The book explains complexity using simple language and easy-to-recognise examples, and suggests pragmatic approaches going forward. Coaches will learn how to expand their scope and impact, and to navigate the new and difficult challenges posed by contemporary businesses. Clients wishing to use coaching in complex change work will learn what to look out for in prospective coaches and how to best deploy them in their organisations.

Coaching in Three Dimensions will appeal greatly to all coaches, including those working with organisations, students and those in training, as well as Human Resources and Organisational Development professionals and senior leaders.

Paul Lawrence, Ph.D., lectures in business coaching at the Sydney Business School (University of Wollongong, Australia) and conducts research into coaching and change. He coaches individuals, teams and groups, and has over 3,000 coaching hours. Before becoming a professional coach/consultant, Paul had a long corporate career, heading up businesses in Spain, Portugal, Japan and Australia. He is President of the NSW Chapter of the International Coaching Federation.

Allen Moore, Ph.D., heads the executive coaching practice for Korn Ferry Hay Group, providing leadership and development consultancy to the world's largest companies. His early corporate career was international marketing for medical devices, then consulting in strategy and change across multiple industry sectors. Allen has worked with more than 10,000 leaders in 450 client companies, in more than 50 countries around the world.

Essential Coaching Skills and Knowledge
Series Editors: Stephen Palmer, Averil Leimon & Gladeana McMahon

The **Essential Coaching Skills and Knowledge** series provides an accessible and lively introduction to key areas in the developing field of coaching. Each title in the series is written by leading coaches with extensive experience and has a strong practical emphasis, including illustrative vignettes, summary boxes, exercises and activities. Assuming no prior knowledge, these books will appeal to professionals in business, management, human resources, psychology, counselling and psychotherapy, as well as students and tutors of coaching and coaching psychology.

www.routledge.com/series/ECS

Titles in the series:

Essential Business Coaching
Averil Leimon, François Moscovici & Gladeana McMahon

Achieving Excellence in Your Coaching Practice: How to Run a Highly Successful Coaching Business
Gladeana McMahon, Stephen Palmer & Christine Wilding

A Guide to Coaching and Mental Health: The Recognition and Management of Psychological Issues
By Andrew Buckley & Carole Buckley

Essential Life Coaching Skills
Angela Dunbar

101 Coaching Strategies
Edited By Gladeana McMahon & Anne Archer

Group and Team Coaching
Christine Thornton

Coaching Women to Lead
Averil Leimon, François Moscovici & Helen Goodier

Developmental Coaching: Life Transitions and Generational Perspectives
Edited by Stephen Palmer & Sheila Panchal

Cognitive Behavioural Coaching in Practice: An Evidence Based Approach
Edited by Michael Neenan & Stephen Palmer

Brief Coaching: A Solution Focused Approach
Chris Iveson, Evan George & Harvey Ratner

Interactional Coaching
Michael Harvey

Solution Focused Coaching in Practice
Bill O'Connell, Stephen Palmer & Helen Williams

Coaching with Meaning and Spirituality
Peter Hyson

Creating a Coaching Culture for Managers in Your Organisation
Edited by Dawn Forman, Mary Joyce and Gladeana McMahon

Essential Career Transition Coaching Skills
Caroline Talbott

Group and Team Coaching: The Secret Life of Groups, Second Edition
Christine Thornton

Coaching in Three Dimensions: Meeting the Challenges of a Complex World
Paul Lawrence & Allen Moore

The Heart of Coaching Supervision: Working with Reflection and Self-Care
Eve Turner and Stephen Palmer

Coaching in Three Dimensions

Meeting the Challenges of a Complex World

Paul Lawrence and Allen Moore

LONDON AND NEW YORK

First published 2019
by Routledge
2 Park Square, Milton Park, Abingdon, Oxon OX14 4RN

and by Routledge
711 Third Avenue, New York, NY 10017

Routledge is an imprint of the Taylor & Francis Group, an informa business

British Library Cataloguing in Publication Data
A catalogue record for this book is available from the British Library

Library of Congress Cataloging in Publication Data
Names: Lawrence, Paul, 1963- author. | Moore, Allen, 1956- author.
Title: Coaching in three dimensions : meeting the challenges of a complex
    world / Paul Lawrence & Allen Moore.
Description: Abingdon, Oxon ; New York, NY : Routledge, 2018.
Identifiers: LCCN 2018011846 (print) | LCCN 2018014678 (ebook) | ISBN
    9781351233118 (Master e-book) | ISBN 9780815378112 (hardback) |
    ISBN 9780815378136 (pbk.)
Subjects: LCSH: Executive coaching. | Personal coaching.
Classification: LCC HD30.4 (ebook) | LCC HD30.4 .L39 2018 (print) | DDC
    658.3/124—dc23
LC record available at https://lccn.loc.gov/2018011846

ISBN: 978-0-8153-7811-2 (hbk)
ISBN: 978-0-8153-7813-6 (pbk)
ISBN: 978-1-351-23311-8 (ebk)

Typeset in New Century Schoolbook
by Swales & Willis Ltd, Exeter, Devon, UK

MIX
Paper from
responsible sources
FSC   FSC® C013056
www.fsc.org

Printed and bound in Great Britain by
TJ International Ltd, Padstow, Cornwall

Contents

Acknowledgements   xv
Foreword   xvii

Introduction   1

The three dimensions   4

Coaching APPROACH   9

1   The traditional approach   11

2   The dialogic approach   19

3   The systemic approach   44

Coaching PRACTICE   61

4   A systemic approach to coaching
individuals   63

5   Coaching teams and groups   80

6   Coaching the organisation   105

Coach DEVELOPMENT   123

7   Competence   125

8 Capability   129

9 Perspective   133

   Experience and reflection   153
   Last thoughts   161
   Index   162

Acknowledgements

So many people helped us write this book.

The first draft of this book looked very different. Unrecognisable. In a sense, what is written here has emerged from all the various conversations we've engaged in with others. It has been co-created, and is an example of change in action.

We began by calling coaches, asking them what innovations they had built into their own practice or seen in others. Whilst we don't remember everyone we spoke to, that list included people like Josie McLean, Tiffany Missiha, Patti Gwynne, Janet Feldman, Margaret Philips, Wayland Lum, Tanya Harris, Andreas Priestland, Rebecca Merrill, Tom Loncar, Tim Rossi, Anne Bartlett, Noelene Kelly, Virginia Mansell, Kathy McKenzie, Kieran White, Amanda Horne, Simone Sietsma, Jo Fisher, Elise Sernik, Melissa Rosenthal, Monica Cable, Eva Freedman, Kate Morten, Sheryl Brosnan, Edna McKelvey, Marisa Dantanarayana, Helen Williams and Yvonne McLean.

When we started writing the book, we shared early drafts with friends and colleagues, all of whom gave us wonderful feedback. Those people included Andreas Priestland and Melissa Rosenthal again, Catherine Turco, Susan Harry, Tatiana Bachkirova, Gordon Spence, Genevieve Vignes, Renata Hodges, Denis Healy, Graeme Reid, Floris Rommerts, John Raymond, Geoff Abbott, Amy Miszalski, Holly Cole-Havens, Padraig O'Sullivan, Nicole Toohey and Raechel Gavin.

And of course, none of this would have been possible without having spent quite a few years as coaches. Those who inspired us on our journeys include Ann Whyte and the WhyteCo coaches, Michael Cavanagh, Anthony Grant, Sean O'Connor, David Clutterbuck, Jennifer Garvey Berger, Robert Kegan, Tatiana Bachkirova, Peter Jackson, David Drake, David Lane, Peter Hawkins, Ken Gergen, Grace McCarthy, all the students at Sydney Business School and pretty much everyone else we've worked with in this wonderful industry.

We would also like to acknowledge the role our families have played in helping us through what has been a long labour. So, thanks to Sangwan, Alexander, MacKenzie, Ruth, Charlotte, Callum, Cameron and Ashleigh.

Foreword

Some books are braver than others. Some push delicately at
a field or an idea, nudging it gently so that the reader is led
to a new idea or two like a comfortable walk down a marked
pathway, no big surprises, nothing dangerous ahead. Other
books, like this one, barrel past the boundaries of a field,
pushing down the fences and scattering the sacred cows.
These books might leave readers uncomfortable and even
lost sometimes, as the familiar shapes they expect don't
materialise and the landscape looks unfamiliar and strange.
But really, what's the point of a book? To leave you comfortable in the way you have been already? Or to shake you up
so that new ideas settle in and make what you used to do
seem somehow smaller than what you'll do next?

Nearly twenty years ago, Catherine Fitzgerald asked
me to co-edit a book, *Executive Coaching: Practices and
Perspectives*. Our book, one of the first of its kind, aimed
to offer a very wide view on this emerging field and we
sought to make sense of what it was and what the field
might become. Nearly 20 years later, the field is massive
and books abound, with various practitioners and researchers trying to help coaches progress in this or that aspect of
coaching. But few of those books take as radical and sweep-
ing a look as *Coaching in Three Dimensions*. This book will
go to the very heart of your practice, making you ask questions perhaps you haven't asked yourself in a while: What
is coaching, anyway? What are its boundaries? What are its
highest hopes? And who am I, as the coach?

In a world growing more complex for the leaders we coach, it makes sense that our work as coaches should be more complex too. But what does that even mean in our field? Paul and Allen offer us a set of choices we might not have noticed we were making – in our approach, in our practice and in our own professional development. They offer us three different options in each domain and illustrate those options with stories from their own practice and the practice of others they have researched. Some of the distinctions will make you think, others might make you squirm a little as they push against what has been coaching dogma for the last two decades. You might find things you delight in as well as things you disagree with. But I bet it will be hard to read this book without reaching the ultimate goal that Paul and Allen want more than anything: your increasing sense of curiosity about what's possible for you and for your clients – and for the entire field of coaching. If you believe, as I do, that coaching is a critical support to the future of our organisations, and that organisations are a critical support to the future of our planet, you need to read this book and understand what the future of coaching might look like. Along the way, you might find a new set of possibilities in yourself.

Jennifer Garvey Berger

Author of *Changing on the Job* and *Simple Habits for Complex Times*.

Introduction

Jill the coach meets Adam the coachee, having been told beforehand that Adam needs to be more influential. What does Jill do in that first meeting? We could consider an answer in terms of favourite models: cognitive-behavioural, solutions-focused, narrative, etc. . . ., but knowing her choice of model doesn't help us understand how Jill navigates complexity. The traditional approach would be for Jill to focus squarely on Adam's needs. Jill's relationship with the organisation may not extend outside the coaching room, as she helps Adam work out for himself what it means to be more influential and to put in place an action plan. This is a common approach, but how effective is it likely to be if Adam's predicament is more layered and complex than it first appears?

A friend of ours went to a conference recently, attended by company directors. The speakers talked about how complex the world has become and how, as a consequence, long-term planning horizons have shrunk from ten years to three years at most. They talked about change being the new normal and how there is no longer such a thing as business-as-usual. They talked about the need for boards to have more conversations that reflect the nature of the world today; volatile, uncertain, complex and ambiguous (VUCA). If boards need to spend more time reflecting on the complex nature of the world today, what do coaches need to do? Coaching, as an industry, has been around a while. How is it adapting to the demands of an increasingly complex world? Are coaches coaching differently? Are purchasers thinking differently about what coaching means to their organisations? We see some people and organisations adapting, and many not.

The traditional approach to coaching still prevails, but traditional approaches fail to take into account how organisations really work. Organisations comprise tangled webs of multiple, ever-shifting, relationships. What happens in one part of the organisation impacts on what happens somewhere else in the organisation, and the nature of this process is unpredictable. Jill the coach might help Adam learn new skills. Adam might invest time in understanding the needs of others, and in speaking more confidently in public. But will this help him be more 'influential' if Adam's real issue is that his line manager is failing in his role, and has set unrealistic expectations for the team? And what will happen next month when the new CEO arrives, the one who fired Adam's boss from his previous role?

The traditional approach to coaching assumes we can best serve organisations by focusing our energies on individuals, changing the world one person at a time. This mission fits well with the aspirations of our colleagues in organisational development, those who look to individual leaders to become heroes, providing direction and inspiration to others. But what if this isn't enough? What if efforts to change the world person-by-person don't work? Coaching has been traditionally defined in terms of a one-to-one relationship between coach and coachee. But what if we ought to be focusing less on individuals and more on patterns of relationships? A growing demand for group and team coaching suggests that organisations are beginning to recognise the limitations of the individual paradigm for change and the need to focus on group dynamics.

We will spend more time with Jill and Adam in this book, exploring different *approaches* to coaching, different forms of *practice* and different strategies for coach *development*. We call these the three dimensions for coaching amidst complexity. *Coaching in Three Dimensions* is our attempt to explain complexity using simple language, and to provide practical insight as to how coaches can develop their practice to become more *systemic*. We hope that clients, thinking about how to best use coaching in their organisations, will gain new insight into what to look out for in prospective coaches and how to best deploy them.

In describing the three dimensions in more detail and attempting to bring them to life with practical examples, we challenge the idea that coaching is all about goal setting and action plans. We challenge the idea that coaching is best described as one person coaching another. We challenge the idea that becoming a better coach is all about acquiring new skills. We offer this three-dimensional perspective on coaching in the hope it will be of practical use to those of us who believe we need to think differently about coaching if coaching is to remain relevant. The world is changing, so must we. If coaching as an industry is to continue being relevant, then we suggest we must all:

- Start embracing ambiguity and uncertainty and stop always trying to simplify.
- Start trying to understand and stop trying to prove.
- Start becoming more adaptive and systemic and stop obsessing on becoming 'professional'.

Above all perhaps, we need to get (even more) curious.

Paul & Allen

The three dimensions

The structure of this book and a process to guide you in further defining 'who am I as a coach' are represented in Figure A.1. It's based on a stack of theory, years of experience, and conversations with more people than we can remember. We're excited about it. To try and best spread that excitement we've avoided too many direct references to

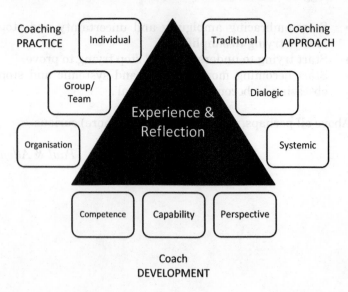

Figure A.1 Coaching in Three Dimensions

theory. Instead we've annotated like mad and included a list of references and comments at the end of each chapter. We suggest you first read each chapter through without paying attention to the endnotes, and then refer to an endnote only if you want to delve deeper afterwards.

This book is divided into four sections. The first three sections of this book provide an account of the three dimensions. Coaches, we invite you to reflect upon your self-as-coach in the context of these dimensions and to consider the following questions:

1   What is your current approach to coaching?
2   What forms of coaching do you practise?
3   Who are you becoming as a coach?

In the final chapter, we invite you to consider the role of reflective practice, or supervision, in your development as coach.

Purchasing clients, we invite you to come up with a different sort of plan, based on a different way of looking at change and new criteria for choosing the coaches you want to help you.

The 3D model encourages us to think about the **approach** we take to coaching. The approach we adopt will tend to define the nature of our coaching **practice**, and will likely reflect the way we think about our own **development**.

First dimension – Coaching APPROACH

In the first part of the book we explore different approaches to coaching. The **traditional** approach is based on conventional wisdom. Coaching is positioned as a set of skills and competencies, defined primarily with the one-to-one coaching relationship in mind. The coach likely sees their role as being to help the coachee come up with solutions; by defining goals and holding the coachee accountable to achieving those goals. The **dialogic** coach has a different understanding as to how coaching works. The idea of dialogue is simple;

listening without prejudice and saying what needs to be said. When two people engage in dialogue, they co-create; new possibilities emerge. The dialogic coach has a different view as to the importance of self-awareness and the relevance of goals, and a different understanding as to the role of listening. To the dialogic coach, listening without judgement creates a space in which genuinely new and unexpected insights and solutions may emerge. The **systemic** coach is not only comfortable working with dialogue, but also notices and works with patterns of dialogue. To understand a coachee's issue, systemic coaches seek to understand the nature of the system in which the coachee is operating. They pay attention not only to immediate relationships, but to achieving a holistic perspective of the organisation and its environment. To a systemic coach the hierarchy is a terribly simplistic representation of the way the organisation works.

Second dimension – Coaching PRACTICE

In the second part of the book we review different aspects of practice. We start with **individual** coaching and consider the different approaches likely to be adopted by traditional, dialogic and systemic coaches. Then we consider **team and group** coaching and discuss how a dialogic approach may enable the coach to work more effectively with groups, and how the systemic approach may be essential for working with teams across a wide range of situations and contexts. Finally, we look at how the coaching practitioner can add value at the **organisational** level. We consider different approaches to building 'coaching cultures', and ask – what are the critical differences between successful and less successful approaches to working in this domain? Again, we suggest that coaches with a systemic approach may be particularly effective working in this space.

Third dimension – Coach DEVELOPMENT

The approaches we adopt and the practices we prefer, are reflections of the way we think about our own development.

First, we consider a focus on **competence**, and acquiring new skills. Second, we consider **capability**. To focus on capability includes the acquisition of new skills, but includes also our quality of thinking, self-awareness and commitment to learning. Third, we consider vertical development. To develop vertically is to access new ways of looking at the world, to acquire new **perspectives**, to develop new relationships with complexity.

In the final chapter, we share our thoughts on reflective practice. We don't become more skilful nor more capable, nor more adept at navigating complexity, without doing stuff. If you agree, then your development plan is likely constructed around new experiences, trying new stuff out. Experience by itself however, rarely leads to significant breakthrough. We must make the time to reflect upon those experiences and to learn from them. In this final chapter, we consider the value of coaching supervision. The word 'supervision' used in a coaching context, means different things to different people. We define it essentially as reflective practice. We suggest that supervision has a useful role to play in any coach's development plan, but that role will be different depending on where you are in your development journey. The purpose of this last chapter is to help the coach be clear as to the role of supervision in their development plan, to choose the right supervisor, and to contract most effectively with that supervisor. If you are a purchaser of coaching services, then you may usefully reflect on where the provision of opportunities for reflective practice fits in your coaching strategy.

Coaching APPROACH

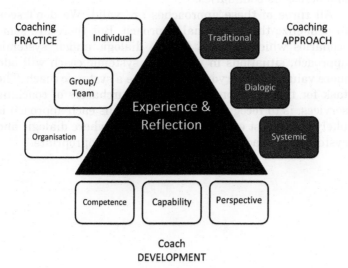

Coaching PRACTICE

- Individual
- Group/ Team
- Organisation

Experience & Reflection

Coaching APPROACH

- Traditional
- Dialogic
- Systemic

Competence   Capability   Perspective

Coach DEVELOPMENT

Traditional coaches work mostly with individuals. They see their role as helping coachees think things through for themselves. They see themselves as outside agents and don't often encounter others in the client organisation. The best traditional coaches are great listeners, able to empathise and see the world through their coachee's eyes.

Dialogic coaches look at things differently. They see themselves as agents in the coaching process, like it or not, co-creators of whatever insights and intentions emerge from the interaction. They are very aware of their own role in the reflective process, and the extent to which their own listening enables or inhibits divergent thinking.

Systemic coaches are not only comfortable working with dialogue, but are also able to work with patterns of dialogue. They understand that change emerges from the multitude of interactions taking place every day in the client organisation. Systemic coaches take a view of the functioning of the organisation as a whole. The organisation, in this sense, is defined by the patterns of dialogue that take place within and across its boundaries.

All three of these approaches are valid. We don't seek to demonize the traditional approach. But there are some scenarios which call out for the dialogic and/or systemic approach; situations in which the systemic coach will add more value. Not everyone wants to be a systemic coach. The task for the traditional coach, and purchasers of coaching services, is to recognise in which domains each approach is likely to be most effective, and consider where dialogic and systemic approaches may be particularly appropriate.

1

The traditional approach

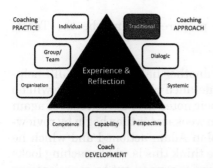

Coaching PRACTICE — Individual

Group/ Team

Organisation

Experience & Reflection

Coaching APPROACH — Traditional

Dialogic

Systemic

Competence — Capability — Perspective

Coach DEVELOPMENT

Picture a small meeting room on the eighth floor of a tall office building. Inside the meeting room sit Adam (a manager) and Jill (a visiting coach). Jill has already had a conversation with the HR manager, who told her Adam needs to get better at influencing. Adam and his line manager have agreed that this is what the coaching needs to be about. Adam and Jill have met once before to talk about the process. Now the coaching begins . . .

Adam:	I want to become more influential.
Jill:	What will it be like after you've become more influential?
Adam:	People will more readily accept my point of view. It will be easier to persuade others to come on the journey. People will seek out my perspective and want to know what I think about certain issues.
Jill:	How influential are you now?
Adam:	Not very, is what it feels like. When I sit in meetings with more senior managers I find it hard to speak up. I'm worried I might say the wrong thing. When I do speak up, sometimes it feels like I'm ignored.

Jill: What could you do differently?

Adam: I could speak up more often *(looks doubtful)*.

Jill: What else?

Adam: I could spend some time preparing in advance for those meetings, think about what I might want to say.

Jill: Any other possibilities occur to you?

Adam: My manager suggested I go to Toastmasters, that I practice projecting my voice with confidence. I know I tend to speak quietly.

Jill: Great! And which of those options do you feel most drawn to?

Adam: Taking time to prepare, and maybe the Toast-masters option.

They carry on talking for another half hour or so, Jill helping Adam come up with a detailed plan as to what he will do next. As they gather up their notes they agree to meet again in three weeks' time. Three weeks later they begin by reviewing what aspects of the plan Adam actioned and which he didn't. Seems familiar? We think this is what coaching looks like much of the time, a service carried out by conscientious well trained 'professionals' with the purpose of helping managers to tackle challenges in the workplace. This traditional approach to coaching is not only popular but, insofar as it is solution-focused, it may often be impactful.[1]

In order to contrast this approach later with both dialogic and systemic approaches, we call your attention to five aspects of traditional coaching.

1   **Two people in the room**

When most people think of coaching they think of coach and coachee, a dyad. If you then prompt people to think about team and group coaching, they may qualify their initial response, but for most people the one-to-one scenario comes first to mind. Some people define coaching exclusively in terms of the one-to-one, or dyadic, relationship.[2] Most coaching associations, including the International Coach Federation (ICF), European Mentoring and Coaching Council (EMCC) and Association for Coaching (AC), focus primarily on dyads.

2 **A strictly confidential conversation**
In researching for this book, we came across an organisational development (OD) manager in a big, well known, organisation. She is responsible for coaching strategy in that organisation. She met an external coach who she knew to be operating in that company. The coach wouldn't tell her who he was coaching. This isn't unusual. One of the ICF codes of ethics reads: 'Maintain the strictest levels of confidentiality with all client and sponsor information unless release is required by law.' Though this is then qualified with the need to 'have a clear agreement about how coaching information will be exchanged among coach, client and sponsor', many coaches interpret this kind of instruction to mean that they shouldn't disclose anything that happens in the coaching room with anyone outside the coaching room. Many coaches, on being asked by someone else in the organisation to provide a commentary on the coaching assignment, will routinely refer the person asking the question back to the coachee. Many traditional coaches restrict their interactions with people in the organisation to their coaching relationships.

3 **'Active' listening**
Notice how the coach doesn't offer any advice. Apart from the single word of encouragement ('great!') Jill sticks to asking questions, mostly open questions. Much of the narrative around contemporary coaching emphasises the importance of listening, sometimes articulated as 'active' listening, or 'Socratic' listening.

4 **Focus on goals**
In the short excerpt above it may be apparent that the coach is working with the GROW model, a popular mnemonic that serves to guide coaches through different

steps in a coaching conversation. The first letter of GROW stands for 'Goal' (the others stand for 'Reality', 'Options' and 'Will'). Goals, and plans to achieve goals, are much referred to in most lists of coaching competencies. The ICF competencies, for example, refer to the coach's ability to:

- Establish a coaching plan and development goals.
- Create a plan with results that are attainable, measurable, specific, and have target dates.
- Keep the client on track by holding attention on the coaching plan and outcomes.
- Positively confront the client with the fact that he/she did not take agreed-upon actions.

The coaching industry places a great emphasis on goals. Goals imply actions. So, in many textbooks we read comments like: 'Without action, the dialogue is just a nice conversation between employee and a concerned manager, not coaching.'[3] The coach is encouraged to ensure that the coachee comes up with a goal early on and that a plan is developed to achieve that goal. Coach and coachee then review progress toward that goal and make changes as required.

5 **Looking forwards not backwards**

One of the ICF core competencies reads: 'Asks questions that move the client forwards toward what they desire, not questions that ask for the client to justify or look backward.' Similarly, some texts seek to differentiate between coaching and counselling/therapy on the basis that coaching looks forwards and counselling/therapy looks backwards. Such a mantra is consistent with solutions-focused approaches to coaching, some of whose advocates would argue that to spend a lot of time on the past is to waste time and energy.[4] Also with research that suggests that rumination on negative thoughts may be associated with anxiety, depression and poor problem- solving ability.[5]

A focus on individuals

These traditional aspects of coaching have become heavily codified. They show up clearly in most versions of coaching core competencies. That coaching has evolved in this way may be the consequence of an unwitting alliance between early practitioners and paying clients, both of whom were happy to support the evolution of coaching primarily as a one-to-one conversation.

Consider the client perspective. Many clients are OD professionals. The traditional approach to OD has been to focus on the realisation of *individual* potential while concurrently reviewing obstacles to that *individual* potential being realised.[6] Moreover, coaching in the early days was often remedial, and so people didn't always want others to know they were being 'coached'. Confidentiality was paramount.

Many of the early coaches were psychologists, therapists and counsellors. Not all these folks worked in organisations and their practice models were largely individualistic. They brought with them a strong belief in the importance of confidentiality. At the same time, they were challenged to explain how coaching was different to therapy. From those discussions emerged a focus on future outcomes, a mantra that plays beautifully into an organisational desire for a clear line of sight linking coaching to performance.

Most coaching research focuses on the extent to which coaching impacts the individual. Did the coachee believe they got good value out of the coaching? To what extent did the coachee achieve their goals? Is the coachee a happier and healthier person? In the 2001 'Manchester study', the authors reported a 570% return on financial investment in a coaching programme.[7] They calculated the figure by interviewing *individuals* who had been coached. There exists little research exploring the impact of coaching on the organisation as a whole.[8]

Be aware that this focus on the leader-as-individual is being challenged more and more. Recent writings on change theory and relational leadership lead us to question the degree to which this paradigm is useful. The extent to which the intentions and actions of an individual really determine what happens in an organisation will always be unclear. Some writers challenge the notion of individual leadership. They emphasise instead the more relational and interactive aspects of leadership. In a 'complex adaptive system' outcomes emerge from the interactions between people. Leaders may influence but they don't control. How many leaders really understand the extent to which the attainment of their individual goals have the desired impact on the functioning of the broader organisational system?

A focus on externals

Traditional coaches are still, usually, depicted as externals rather than managers inside organisations having conversations with their staff. The drive for professionalism may be a factor in this. While coach and coachee tend to come together in a single specific context – a scenario in which the coachee has asked the coach to help him think through a pressing issue – the line manager is likely to engage with his team in a multitude of difference scenarios, many of which will emerge in the same conversation. How hard would it be to establish a single set of rules by which to conduct such a conversation? So, the traditional coach is still usually depicted as an external practitioner while the various coaching institutions continue to work out how they can adapt their frameworks to more readily accommodate the internal employee.

We imagine some of you may be saying to yourselves, yes – and isn't this traditional approach what coaching is all about? To you, we say that we think this approach is both appropriate and valid in many contexts, but it may not serve the coach so well in more complex scenarios. Curious? Read on.

Notes

1 Recent meta-reviews on the efficacy of coaching include: [Grant. A.M. (2013). The efficacy of coaching, In: Passmore, J., Peterson, D.B., & Freire, T. (Eds.) *The Wiley-Blackwell Handbook of the*

Psychology of Coaching and Mentoring, Wiley: UK], [Theeboom, T., Beersma, B. & van Vianen, A.E.M. (2014). Does coaching work? A meta-analysis on the effects of coaching on individual level outcomes in an organisational context. *The Journal of Positive Psychology*, 9(1), 1–18] and [Grover, S., & Furnham, A. (2016). Coaching as a developmental intervention in organisations: A systematic review of its effectiveness and the mechanisms underlying it. *PLoS ONE*, 11(7): 10.1371/journal. pone.0159137].

2 In Vikki Brock's 2014 history of coaching [*Sourcebook of Coaching History*, 2nd edition] she tells the story of how Werner Erhard hosted an historic gathering of coaching pioneers in 1987, at which they agreed twelve coaching principles, one of which was that coaching is a relationship between two people. More recently, in 2010, Grant, Cavanagh, Parker & Passmore also suggested that professional coaching might be usefully defined as a dyadic relationship. Working at the group and organisational level, they suggested, might usefully be defined as the domain of organisational development and HR. See [Grant, A.M., Cavanagh, M.J., Parker, H.M. & Passmore, J. (2010). The state of play in coaching today: A comprehensive review of the field. *An International Review of Industrial & Organizational Psychology*, 25, 125–167].

3 For example, [Emerson, B. & Loehr, A. (2008). *A Manager's Guide to Coaching*. AMACOM: New York].

4 Cavanagh, M. & Grant, A.M. (2010). The solution-focused approach to coaching. In: Cox, E. Bachkirova, T. & Clutterbuck. C. (Eds.) *The Complete Handbook of Coaching*. Sage: London.

5 Nolen-Hoeksema, S. (1998). The other end of the continuum: The costs of rumination. *Psychological Inquiry*, 9(3), 216–219.

6 Lots and lots of references here, many from the *Journal of Change Management*. One of our favourites is [Werkman, R. (2010). Reinventing organization development: How a sense-making perspective can enrich OD theories and interventions. *Journal of Change Management*, 10(4), 421–438].

7 The Manchester study was a piece of work published in the *Manchester Review* [McGovern, J., Lindermann, M., Vergara, M.A., Murphy, S., Barker, L., & Warrenfelz, R. (2001). Maximizing the impact of executive coaching: Behavioral change, organizational outcomes and return on investment. *Manchester Review*, 6(1), 1–9]. The researchers asked subjects to estimate the financial impact of the coaching they received and came up with an average of 570%. Subsequent studies reported similar numbers and there is now an institute whose function it is to help practitioners come up with their own return-on-investment models [http://www.roiinstitute.net/]. Anthony Grant, Director of the

Coaching Psychology Unit at Sydney University, critiques these formulaic attempts to quantify the impact of coaching in financial terms. He suggests instead that practitioners look instead to metrics around well-being and goal attainment, outcomes for which there exist available validated measures. But these measures are still mostly individualistic. See [Grant, A.M. (2012). ROI is a poor measure of coaching success: towards a more holistic approach using a well-being and engagement framework. *Coaching: An International Journal of Theory, Research and Practice*. 5(2), 72–85].

8 See, for example [Grant, A.M., Cavanagh, M.J., Parker, H.M. & Passmore, J. (2010). The state of play in coaching today: A comprehensive review of the field. *An International Review of Industrial & Organizational Psychology*, 25, 125–167].

2

The dialogic approach

In a parallel universe, Jill the coach has a different approach to coaching. She goes into the session thinking about dialogue, and what she can do to create a space in which Adam is comfortable exploring aloud whatever he wants to talk about. She doesn't go into the session thinking she must help Adam identify a goal, or that she can only ask questions, or that she should encourage Adam to focus immediately on actions. Jill and Adam have a different conversation.

Adam: I want to become more influential.

Jill: What does influential mean?

Adam: It means that people will more readily accept my point of view. It will be easier to persuade others to come on the journey. People will seek out my perspective and want to know what I think about certain issues.

Jill: I've just caught sight of a picture in my mind. The Dalai Lama sat cross-legged in front of an attentive audience. . .

Adam: Hmm *(looks doubtful)*. I don't expect everyone to agree with everything I say. I think it's more about me believing that I'm talking good sense. I want to get involved, be informed and feel more confident.

Jill: Now I have a picture of you walking around talking to people, watching what they do, listening to what they say, accumulating a kind of wisdom. . .

Adam: Yes! Correct.

Jill: When have you felt like that before?

Adam: Well, in my last role. I reported into a steering committee. I went to every meeting well prepared and presented clear recommendations. They almost always agreed with what I suggested. Sometimes they didn't, but that was OK. Sometimes they saw something that I didn't, but they always took my opinion seriously.

Jill: You made time to think about what you would say and they respected you for that.

Adam: Yes, and they made time to listen. There was a structure that gave me regular access to senior management and because everyone else knew I was the project leader everyone cooperated with me and did what I needed them to do.

Jill: You respected them and they respected you and others in the organisation respected you for your place in the hierarchy. Is that part of it?

Adam: It is! I believe in hierarchy and in being organised. In this new role, it's so much harder. There's no steering committee; I'm not even sure who I should be engaging with. No one can tell me. I asked my line manager but he just told me I need to speak up more when I'm in meetings with senior management. That doesn't really help because I don't see them all that often and I don't know that it will make that much difference. Everyone is so busy! I can't persuade anyone to commit to what I want them to do. They nod and agree but don't deliver and I don't like pushing back because I know that will only lead to conflict.

Jill: With structure comes harmony . . .

Adam: . . . it's something about working out who are the
            key players in this whole project and getting to
            know them. Then finding a way of holding others
            to account for the work they're supposed to deliver,
            and doing all that without relying on my line man-
            ager. He's so busy too I hardly ever get to see him.

Notice the difference between this conversation and the earlier one. In the first conversation Jill skipped lightly across
Adam's answers, and moved quickly to what Adam might do
next. There are scenarios in which the first approach may
add great value, in which Adam is grateful to rattle through
a few options and come up with an action plan. Managers
have lots of conversations like this with their colleagues
every day, useful conversations from which the person being
coached walks away with new clarity of purpose. There
will be times though when such a conversation isn't so useful. This may be one such example; it appears that Adam's
dilemma is more complex than it first seemed.

   One difference between the two scenarios, we suggest, is
the way Jill is listening. In both cases Jill may be said to be
'actively' listening. In the first conversation, she is attending
to Adam's point of view, asking questions and listening to
the answers. At no point does she resist his thinking or offer
advice of her own. It's Adam who's begun painting a picture
of what 'being influential' will look like. It's Adam who has
identified how he feels, and Adam who has come up with all
the options as to what he might do next. It's only in comparing the two conversations that we are led to consider that
Adam may not have explored the issue in sufficient depth
in the first conversation to come up with a solution to which
he is truly committed. It's sometimes useful to imagine the
coachee as an iceberg. The 30 per cent above water is readily
visible – the person's actions, behaviours and words – but
70 per cent sits below the water line – intentions, beliefs,
assumptions, values and sense of identity. 'Active listening'
may attend to the 30 per cent, but it requires a different *way*
of listening to understand what else is going on.

In the first conversation, though she's listening intently to Adam's every word, Jill may be listening less keenly to his underlying intentions. When Adam says he wants to be more influential, Jill doesn't to stop to consider what he really means. She assumes she knows what Adam is trying to say, that the word 'influential' has only one meaning. She kicks on quickly to the next phase of the conversation. When Adam says he finds it hard to speak up in meetings with senior managers, again she doesn't stop to explore further. Instead she asks Adam about possible solutions. Jill is actively listening to the words, but we're curious about what's going on for her. She's moving fast, following a process and looking to land some actions. Whether she's aware of it or not, she appears to be being driven by an agenda along the lines of 'it's my job to help you come up with a goal and a plan'. Not surprising really, when so many coaching texts emphasise the importance of goals and plans. But this approach may be limiting the extent to which she will be helpful to Adam.

In the second scenario, notice how Jill pays more attention to the meaning of the words Adam uses. She stops to explore that meaning. She doesn't assume she knows what he means when he says he wants to be more 'influential'. She asks him what he means, and plays back what she thinks he is trying to say. She seems less interested in the literal meaning of the words he uses, more interested in who Adam is being; his identity. Does he also have a picture in mind of the Dalai Lama as he's speaking, or is Jill off the mark? This first attempt to understand what he is trying to say *does* miss the mark. The picture of Adam walking around and talking to people is closer. She notices something about respect and hierarchy too, this line of enquiry taking them both away from a single definition of the word 'influential' into something more layered; something that Adam himself wants to think harder about. It's not simply that Jill has bought a different book of coaching questions. The difference is that Jill appears more curious in the second scenario, more intent upon understanding who Adam is, what matters to him, and how he makes meaning of the world. Her listening feels 'cleaner', less agenda-driven. In the context of this chapter we'll say that her approach is less *monologic* and more *dialogic*. Which begs the question, what exactly do we mean by these terms?

Monologue and dialogue

Dialogue is one of many words in the English language that has a multitude of meanings. Here's one definition of dialogue taken from a coaching textbook:

> Dialogue is a conversation in which both parties are seeking understanding. They are not trying to prove, teach, or motivate the other to do something. Coaching is a conversation in which the coach attempts to understand, and thereby helps the coachee to understand, what and how it is that the coachee is blocking their own success.[1]

We think this sentence is contradictory. On the one hand, it says that a dialogue is a conversation in which the coach isn't trying to motivate anyone to do something. On the other hand, it says that the coach's role is to help the coachee understand how she is blocking her own success. This implies that should the coachee say anything that doesn't appear to be advancing the agenda toward an identification of blockers, then the coach is likely to bring the conversation back toward that outcome. Furthermore, it's not clear on whose terms the coach is trying to understand the coachee. Does the coach have an internal checklist of factors that get in the way of success? Is that what the coach is listening for? Or is the coach operating without an agenda, seeking to understand the coachee on the coachee's terms? This definition of dialogue sounds more like monologue in the way that we define the terms. Confused? We will try and explain.

Adam Kahane[2] has helped organisations all over the world solve intractable problems. He played a role in helping South Africa transition out of apartheid. He worked with politicians, guerrilla groups, business people and citizens in Colombia, helping them to think together about a new future for their country. He helped leaders in Argentina fix a broken justice system. He worked with academics, NGOs, businesses, government, journalists, trade unionists, ex-guerrillas and clergy in Guatemala to create together a new national vision. In each case, what he brought to the table was dialogue. People arrived at these forums with clearly determined points of views. The most likely outcome in each case was that the participants would debate whose version of the truth was the universal truth. Kahane had to work hard to avoid this scenario, otherwise all he would have succeeded in doing would have been to create a space in which multiple universal truths came into conflict. To engage in dialogue requires letting go of the notion that we know what the answer is.

As individuals, we have no direct, privileged access to reality or truth. Our version of reality is constructed through our perceptions and the way we each make meaning of our experiences. To engage in dialogue is to let go of certainty. Dialogue is about exploring, making room for multiple perspectives and multiple truths. In dialogue, each participant offers a perspective, *and* remains open to others' perspectives. Through this co-creative process, new possibilities emerge that were not there before.

Dialogue, as we define it, is not the same as conversation. William Isaacs[3] makes a clear distinction (Figure 2.1). He defines a conversation as *any* kind of verbal exchange. There are different forms of conversation each of which may be most appropriate in a particular context. *Dialogue*, he says, is fundamentally different to *skilled conversation* and *debate*. To engage in dialogue is to listen without parameters, without a pre-determined sense of what's reasonable and what's not. It's about coming to the conversation suspending pre-conceived notions, pre-determined ideas and any sense of knowing best. This in contrast to most of the conversations in which we engage, in which we have a pre-determined sense of what it's OK to say and think. To engage in dialogue, as defined here, is hard for a traditional coach. It means, for example, holding at arm's length all notions and ideas of what a coach is supposed to do. The coach's attempts to engage in dialogue may be thwarted by, for example, a suppressed desire to offer advice, a determination to come up with a goal or an action plan, or a belief that the coach is ultimately responsible for ensuring the coachee finds a solution to their issue.

According to the model, we make a fundamental choice before engaging in any verbal exchange. Either we choose to defend a pre-determined position or we choose to vacate that position and admit an unlimited number of possibilities. If we choose not to vacate our position then we are preparing ourselves to engage in *skilful conversation*, a *controlled discussion* or *debate*. These kinds of conversation need not feel antagonistic or tense. The more skilled we are at negotiating, the more able we are to self-regulate, the easier and more effective these exchanges become. But that doesn't mean we are engaged in dialogue. These are all monologic forms of interacting. Let us illustrate.

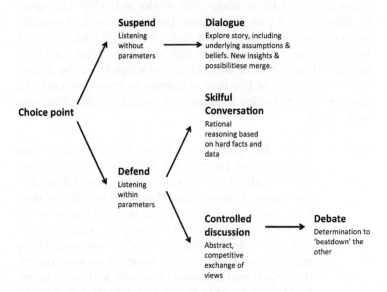

Figure 2.1

Controlled discussion/debate

Jill is back coaching Adam. Adam is unhappy with his work-life balance.

Adam: I'm unhappy about my work-life balance. I'm working long hours and finding life stressful. Despite working really hard, it doesn't feel like I'm achieving anything. I'm trying to manage a bunch of projects all at the same time, failing to do a great job with any of them. My team are unhappy because I don't spend enough time with them setting direction. My peers are unhappy because I miss deadlines and don't get back to their messages. My line manager is unhappy because results are mediocre. Even my partner is unhappy because she doesn't get to see enough of me, and she says that even when I am around, I'm cranky.

After listening for a while, Jill works out what the issue is. She hears Adam talk about the 600 unopened e-mails in his inbox. She hears him talk about eight big projects he is leading. She hears him talk about his team and how unclear they are as to what they are supposed to be doing. She is reminded of her own struggles to prioritise early in her career. She begins to share her insights with Adam who nods slowly.

Jill: There are some tools I can share to help you manage your inbox more skilfully and some suggestions about restructuring your e-mail files. But you know, I have a pet theory based on my own experiences that no one can be working on more than three priorities at a time. My suggestion is that you reflect regularly on what are your three main priorities. Once you are clear on your priorities, you'll find it easier to engage with your team. You'll also be able to get home earlier in a more relaxed frame of mind.

Adam stops nodding and pulls a face.

Adam: It won't work. I can't possibly drop five of the eight
          projects; they are all too important and the busi-
          ness doesn't currently have the means to provide
          additional resource.
Jill: I just wonder about that; are all eight of them so
          equally important?
Adam: You better believe it, they all are . . .

The conversation continues, with Jill listening out for anything Adam says that may support her belief that Adam
needs to do a better job prioritising. Adam intuitively understands what Jill thinks and so is careful not to give her
anything to work with.

They are both listening intently to each other. Jill is listening for evidence that her prioritising theory is correct,
while Adam is listening for anything that confirms his view
that Jill is wrong. Little progress is made because both Jill
and Adam are *defending* a perspective. Jill isn't prepared to
shift from a perspective that says prioritisation is the issue,
and Adam isn't prepared to shift from a perspective that says
prioritisation is *not* the issue. Neither Jill nor Adam fully
realise what's going on. Jill doesn't see herself as 'defending' anything – she is trying to help Adam and is becoming
frustrated at his apparent inability to open his mind to new
possibilities. Adam isn't defending anything either – he's
waiting for Jill to come up with an idea that makes sense.
Meanwhile the conversation continues – politely – but with
ideas being batted back and forth like a ping-pong ball in a
game of table tennis. Adam and Jill are engaged in a *controlled discussion* or *debate*, albeit with understandable
intent and impeccable manners.

Skilled conversation

After the first meeting Jill reflects. She plays back to a
colleague what happened and through their conversation
recognises that she may have over-fixated on one solution.

Rather embarrassed, she recognises her colleague's observation that she seemed to be pushing an agenda. She arrives for the second session determined to be more open-minded, prepared to dig deeper into Adam's arguments. Adam tells her (again) that he can't possibly drop any of the eight projects. Jill picks on one of the projects, an initiative to reduce supplier numbers.

Jill: Help me understand, Adam, why does this project have to be completed this year?

Adam: By reducing the number of suppliers we can save the business half a million dollars in costs.

Jill: Half a million dollars?

Adam: Yes, and the business is counting on those savings. They're already written into the latest forecast.

Jill: So, you feel compelled to make sure those savings get delivered.

Adam: I do. If we don't deliver, then we straightaway lose half a million dollars off our bottom line.

Jill: What would be the worst thing about that?

Adam: The worst thing is that everyone will say it's my fault – here's another project that Adam's failed to deliver.

Jill: So, you're worried that your reputation will take a hit?

Adam: Exactly.

Jill: So, let me play back what I've heard, Adam. You have eight projects on the go. History tells you that you are unlikely to succeed in delivering all eight of them on time and to expectations. Most likely you will deliver some of them reasonably well and others not at all. This is stressful because you feel you're working long hours and yet your reputation is almost certainly going to take another hit.

Adam: That's it.

Jill: This supplier management project could be deferred if it wasn't for the half million-dollar savings?

Adam: I suppose.

Jill: And the business reports its results to the nearest million dollars – am I right?

Adam: Yes.

Jill: So, it's possible that deferring the project will have no noticeable impact on the reported bottom line?

Adam (looks doubtful).

Jill: And if you deferred the project then this would allow you to allocate your energies to other, higher value projects. Not only that, but if you make the case well, you can change people's expectations now as to when the supplier management project is likely to be delivered.

Adam: I suppose.

In this second meeting Jill is demonstrating the extent to which she has been listening to what Adam has been saying. She has succeeded in disentangling fact from feeling and is challenging Adam based on an accurate understanding of the situation. She is doing so skilfully, making sure Adam has an opportunity to agree or disagree at each stage of her argument. She is ready to change direction and explore a different approach if Adam succeeds in proving her wrong. At the end of it all Adam really doesn't have much choice but to agree because she has presented her case so effectively. So, we might argue, Jill has done a great job.

Great job perhaps, but she has not engaged Adam in dialogue. This is still monologue, because however well Jill appears to be listening, she is still defending the same perspective – which is that the answer to Adam's problem is to do a better job prioritising. She may have dropped the idea that Adam ought to focus on just three of the eight projects, and she may be listening intently to every word of Adam's argument, but she is still hanging on to the idea that he needs to prioritise. This is *skilful conversation*, a monologic type of conversation often confused with dialogue. When people talk about 'Socratic listening' this is sometimes what they are referring to, listening with the purpose of finding flaws in the argument.

Jill leaves the session feeling pleased with herself. In the first session Adam didn't agree to do anything whereas in this session he has committed to defer one of the eight projects. So, she is disappointed when she arrives at the next session to find that Adam hasn't followed through on what he said he would do. The eighth project is still live and Adam is still stressed out.

Dialogue

Jill is discouraged and doesn't know what to do next, so she determines to put aside her theories of what Adam needs to do and to make a concerted effort to understand better who this strange person called Adam really is.

Jill: Tell me what happened, Adam?

Adam: I spoke to my line manager about deferring the supplier management project but
he didn't support me. He said that because
we've announced the project we need to follow
through, or else the suppliers will get angry.
We've already asked them to prepare their
submissions to the panel who will ultimately
decide who we will work with long term. So,
I'm back where I was. I still have too many
projects on the go and I still don't know what
to do about it.

Jill: What sense do you make of it all?

Adam   I've got to keep trying is all, but I'm not optimistic.
(shakes his   I just can't keep everyone happy.
head):

Jill: Keeping everyone happy is important?

Adam: Of course, and right now I'm not doing a great
job. My team isn't happy, my colleagues aren't
happy, my boss isn't happy and my partner
isn't happy.

Jill: Help me understand better the importance of keeping everyone happy.

Adam (shrugs):   It's what counts. If everyone's happy with me then I know I've done a good job. I can go home relaxed. I can put my feet up, have a glass of wine and forget about work for a few hours.

Jill: So, to have a happy life yourself you must do all you can to make others happy?

Adam (looks thoughtful):   I suppose. I hadn't really thought of it that way. I guess that's how I was brought up. My father worked hard to make sure we didn't go without and my mother made sure our house was a happy place. If I got angry with my sister or turned up to the dinner table cranky – that wasn't good.

Jill: Everyone did their best to ensure everyone else was happy?

Adam: That's right. I still believe in that. If we all just went the extra mile for each other, then the world would be a happier place.

Jill: Tell me about 'the extra mile'.

Adam: The extra mile is just about being prepared to put yourself out for others. It's about always saying yes, not saying no.

In this third meeting, it's much less apparent that Jill has an agenda other than seeking to understand what matters to Adam in all of this. By succeeding in putting aside her agenda she has created a space for reflective dialogue. Adam is talking through his predicament and appears to be uncovering new aspects of the dilemma he hadn't noticed before. The conversation continues.

Jill: I think I understand. Going the extra mile is about your commitment to others, in service of creating a happy harmonious place. Your parents taught you this and you've lived your life by that credo ever since. But as a strategy it doesn't seem to be working out for you at work right now?

Adam   It's not working out anywhere. My partner isn't happy
(sighs):   and I haven't spent time with friends for weeks. I
              think it works when everyone has separate needs
              and when there's more time. But if I can't be happy
              until everyone else is happy, then I'm never going
              to be happy doing this job. Everyone's got a dif-
              ferent opinion, a different agenda, different needs.
              I'm going to have to make some decisions here
              (looks worried).

So, here are three different approaches that Jill took with
Adam, each of which may be effective in different circum-
stances. The first conversation was evidently monologic.
Adam and Jill quickly entered a debate (or controlled discussion) and nothing was agreed. The second conversation
was less confrontational. Jill was determined not to get
locked into debate and focused on exploring Adam's views
through a logical/rational lens. Accordingly, she demonstrated to Adam the need to defer one of his smaller projects.
Adam agreed but didn't deliver on his commitment. The second conversation is less obviously monologic because both
parties appear to be actively listening to each other, but it
is monologic. Jill's determination to find a solution means
she is still operating from a 'defensive' stance, defending a
belief that says project eight can be postponed, more generally perhaps defending a belief that says there are always
projects that can be postponed. Only the third conversation
is dialogic in that Jill appears genuinely open to any possibility, even the possibility that there is no solution, even
the possibility that Adam declares himself dissatisfied with
the conversation and says she's a terrible coach. From the
dialogue emerges a new insight for Adam, one that *may* lead
to a new way of approaching his desire for a different work-
life balance.

In chatting to experienced coaches around the world as
part of writing this book we came across Floris Rommerts,
an old friend who has worked with William Isaacs. Floris is
based in Europe and has been coaching for many years. For

Floris, as for us, dialogue sits at the heart of coaching. He described this approach to coaching as:

> ... completely model-less. I'm being completely curious with respect to a central theme. It's about creating an open space, offering myself as a dialogic partner with an individual or a team. It's about going further than enquiry, into the inspirational and creative. One session of two hours may be enough for someone's life.

Floris is challenging another aspect of traditional coaching here; that coaching needs to be spread out over a long period. As we will see in Chapter 4, the dialogic approach fully explored may lead us into some surprising spaces.[4]

Dialogue and identity

When we say that change emerges from dialogue, we are referring not only to the coachee's visible behaviours, but also to the coachee's deeper sense of who he or she is. To understand how dialogue enables the evolution of identity, we need to introduce a bit of theory and to deploy some jargon. The theory we'll introduce is called 'social-constructionism'. Don't be put off by the phrase 'social-constructionism'. All it means is that we construct our realities (the *construction-ism* bit) and that we do so in relationship with other people (the *social* bit). Think about traffic lights. There is nothing implicitly meaningful about a red light, but in some societies we have decided that a red light means 'stop'. We are also pretty much aligned that a green light means 'go'. We are less aligned as to what 'yellow' means, with some people having decided it means 'speed up' and others having decided it means 'slow down'. Just as we work out among ourselves what the different colour traffic lights mean, so we also decide among ourselves who we are as people. Our identities are socially constructed, multi-faceted and dynamic.[5]

As we proceed through life we are continually recreating ourselves, as we engage in different relationships, with different communities, in different contexts. We have not just one self, but a portfolio of selves; self as parent, child, professional, friend and partner. We engage differently with the doctor, the babysitter, the angry co-worker, and the person coaching our kid's sports team. Our identities are not fixed and singular; they are dynamic and multi-dimensional, subject to the dialogue and relationships we engage in with others.

We recently coached the new CEO of an organisation as he approached his first big meeting with the media. He was anxious and kept saying 'I've never been very good at this sort of thing; I'm not going to show up very well in front of all those people.' After a few meetings, it became apparent that he was well prepared technically and enjoyed great support from his PR team. The dialogue drifted toward his sense of self, who he was being in relation to this situation.

CEO:	I'm nervous, I'm just not a very good speaker, not the type of person who's comfortable being on camera in front of a lot of other people.
Coach:	OK, that's one choice . . . showing up as someone who is nervous, not a good speaker, and not comfortable on camera. Is that the self you want to be in this situation?
CEO (a bit flustered):	What do you mean? It doesn't help at all, that's why I'm nervous. I'm going to look bad, and it won't do the company any good either.
Coach:	Are there times in your life when you aren't nervous, when you are a good speaker and comfortable being in front of others? With family, with your team, with . . .
CEO:	Yes, of course. I've been here 18 years. I have a great relationship with my executive team, with R&D, and with our key investors.
Coach:	So there is a 'you' in there somewhere that comes out sometimes that relates well to other people?

CEO (more   I can see where you're going with this.
relaxed):

Coach: Well then, let's look at it. Who are you? Nobody knows more about the company, its capabilities, its vision, its direction – nobody knows that better than you, and there are a multitude of people who see that 'you' when they look at you. How would it be, showing up as that 'you' in front of the camera?

The CEO left the session with a piece of paper in his pocket that read 'I am the best person possible to make this happen,' and the event went well. The CEO had walked into the coaching session with a range of identities to choose from. In dialogue with the coach, one particular identity emerged anew, re-narrated and re-shaped.

Consider the following quote from a change leader working in an Australian public services organisation. How many identities seem to be at play?

I was the transformation guy, bringing a modern way of thinking to a bureaucratic organisation. But the organisation's mantra was 'we're a family' and I was treated like a drunken Uncle Fester, as an outsider. I was the fire-fighter rather than the architect or builder and I created some of the bushfires without knowing it. In the second year, when people realised I was the glue-man trying to make everyone successful, I tried to turn relationships round using language. It was hard work, forever selling yourself, always in interview mode. Who are you? What makes you so special, as an ex-private sector person? I assembled my team of 'green berets' to come with me on the journey, and they've all been fantastic.

Not only do we have different identities to choose from, but those identities are dynamic, continually evolving as we experience new events, reflect upon how we responded to those events, and decide what meaning to make of those responses. As coaches, we are active participants in co-creating the identities of our coachees, just as they are active participants in co-creating our own identities as coaches. Recently we coached a leader who was wondering – 'am I strategic?' Here's what he shared:

> I like to think I am strategic. I point to the work I did in my last role, focusing on reducing cost to below that of our key competitor so we could invest more in capital projects. In this current role, however, the board is unhappy with our strategy. I'm recommending we cut prices to increase volume and build market share. They want us to raise prices so we can invest in new markets, take advantage of lower levels of competition and build a more resilient business. In the heat of the moment one of the board members told me I was just a cost slasher and didn't have a strategic bone in my body. One of my best friends works at a strategy consulting firm and tells me the board member was talking rubbish. Another friend at a different consulting firm pulled a face and says maybe I should stick to operations. I'm really confused.

We engaged in a dialogue during which he decided that he *did* have had a strong strategic self. He also had a less certain, self-doubting self, who had been roused by a board member who became short-tempered when he didn't get his way, and a somewhat incompetent strategist from a second-rate consulting firm. Before he left, this leader shook our hand and told us we were the best coaches that ever lived, thereby facilitating at least a temporary shift in our view of ourselves as a coach.

Identity is the one of the most frequent topics for coaching among C-suite leaders.[6] You may be familiar with the term 'imposter syndrome',[7] often used to describe people raised to be humble who have risen quickly to the top executive ranks. For these people, their sense of 'who am I' has not yet caught up with the current reality, and they fear others will see them as fake. The coach can add value in these scenarios by creating the environment for dialogue, a process through which new identities may emerge and evolve. Identity is contextual. The coachee's question 'Who am I?' may usefully be re-framed as 'Who am I being *in this context*?'

Dialogue and goal theory

Some years back, few challenged the notion that goal-setting sits at the heart of coaching. Now there's a debate. For example, David Drake[8] writes: 'I have. . . observed that goals are often counter-productive'. Herminia Ibarra[9] writes 'Goals can be problematic because, essentially, they are outcomes. In a complex world, we are due for a critical re-examination of the way we set and pursue goals'.

People who don't like goals seem to object most to how goals are used. Stories abound of organisations exhorting their employees to strive to achieve targets they had no say in. Or of people being asked to come up with goals in an environment where 'soft goals' are quickly challenged. We recently coached someone who had just come from a leadership programme attended by the CEO. At the beginning of the programme every attendee had to come up with a challenging goal, something that would be really difficult to achieve. There was to be a prize awarded to the person who, in the eyes of their colleagues, achieved the most difficult goal. Meantime, the CEO sat and watched while everyone thought about what goal to declare, nodding his satisfaction or shaking his head depending on whether he thought the goal was challenging enough. Many in the group ended up committing to goals they had little confidence in delivering.

There's another reason some people don't like goals. Traditional goal theory assumes that the actions we take are directed by *conscious* goals and intentions.[10] But sometimes people don't know what their goals and intentions are. They come to coaching uncertain, and to expect them to come up with a goal within the first ten minutes of a session isn't going to help. What such people need is a space in which to reflect. If the environment is conducive, then clear intentions will emerge. The ultimate and most obvious examples are people coming to coaching with questions like: 'What do I want to do with my life?' and 'Who do I want to be?' These are big messy questions that take time to explore. Consider the following quote from David Clutterbuck, writing about the inappropriate use of GROW:[11]

> One of my favourite ghastly examples is the coach, who corralled the client into articulating a goal, then ploughed relentlessly on into the R of GROW until the client stopped the conversation, paused and said: 'Actually, my real issue is that I don't feel I have a purpose in my life any more'. The coach nodded sympathetically. 'That's really interesting. I wish we had time to explore that. But let's park it and focus on the issue we started with . . .'

I've spoken to paying clients in the past who are quite clear about what they expect from their coaches. They want to see tangible behavioural change within two or three sessions of an assignment commencing. If they don't see that change happening, then the coach is asked to terminate the assignment and withdraw from the coaching panel. There is a whole body of literature that talks to SMART goals and the importance of making sure coachees have goals that are highly specific and measurable, with clear timelines attached. Sometimes this is effective, often it isn't. It's a paradigm that appeals to the client whose primary objective is make sure the coachee comes up with a detailed development plan. But many of these plans end up not being implemented because the coachee just didn't find the goals to be compelling.

A couple of years ago, we tracked the progress of 11 coachees, speaking to them four times over the course of ten months. Everybody's goals changed and evolved, sometimes dramatically. They changed in response to external factors, such as political and regulatory changes; to organisational factors, such as restructuring and moving roles. Sometimes they changed simply because the coachee spoke to people;

line manager, mentors, peers, team members, senior managers, colleagues etc. . . This points to two important properties of goals, namely that they are *dynamic* and that they are *co-created*. Some of these goals also appeared to be *unconscious*. One person we tracked had an initial goal around career planning. Coach and coachee talked about career planning for a couple of sessions before personal issues arose that were impacting on his ability to function in the workplace. After a couple of months, he had made sufficient progress on those personal issues to able to focus again on his workplace goals. At the end of the assignment he spoke about feeling significantly more confident around his ability to influence people in the workplace. The goal around influencing others in the workplace wasn't there before he took time out to talk about his personal life. Something in those conversations sparked an insight about his leadership in the workplace. It was this initially unconscious goal that he declared to be his biggest breakthrough at the end of the assignment.

So, the dialogic coach is unlikely to subscribe to a traditional approach to goal-setting. While the traditional coach may be comfortable with a linear approach to goal-setting and goal-achievement, and the idea that goal-setting and goal regulation are entirely conscious processes, the dialogic coach is more likely to see goals as emergent. Dialogue leads to new insights, new possibilities and new directions that didn't exist before.

We are reminded here of a past coaching assignment. The paying client expected the coachee and us to come up with a goal after a couple of sessions. While the coachee seemed committed to coaching, turning up to session on time and completing actions, nevertheless she couldn't articulate what she wanted to get out of coaching. Every session touched on a different subject, something live happening at the time. Seven sessions went by and we still didn't have a goal to share with the client. Then at the end of the eighth session the coachee proclaimed that she at last knew what her goal was; 'to establish great relationships by being curious and suspending judgement,' a theme that encapsulated everything we had talked about up until that point. Not only did she declare her goal, but she also declared she didn't need any more coaching. Identifying the goal was the goal.

Two approaches compared

The dialogic approach is different to the traditional approach. The essential difference lies in the coach's view as to how change happens (Figure 2.2). Listening and effective voicing are important to the traditional coach as a means of ensuring understanding. From this traditional perspective, change is personal and the coach needs to first fully understand in order to be able to facilitate individual change. But this notion of coach as helper introduces inequality into the relationship: the helper has something that the coachee does not, something they may choose to bestow. Listening and effective voicing are important in a different way to the dialogic coach, because this form of communication is the very mechanism by which change happens. Change is social, and meaning is co-constructed.

The dialogic approach has other implications besides (Table 2.1). Both traditional and dialogic coaches may spend most of their time coaching individuals. The dialogic coach's

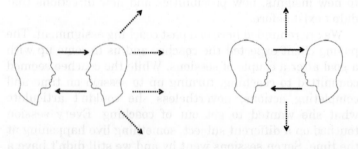

We talk. Coachee decides to change.   We engage in dialogue. Change
                                             emerges from the dialogue.

Traditional   **Dialogic**

Figure 2.2

understanding of dialogue may however enable him to work more effectively with groups. The traditional coach may find group coaching tiring, working hard to establish a dyadic relationship with multiple coachees at the same time. The dialogic coach may find it easier to frame the event as a dialogue in which everyone has a role to play, a role which needs no referencing to professional standards, but only to a propensity to listen and to voice effectively.

The dialogic coach is more likely to contract with a coachee about the shape of confidentiality boundaries than flatly decide that everything discussed in the coaching room may not be discussed outside the room. If change emerges from dialogue, then every dialogue is an opportunity to advance a change agenda. Furthermore, the dialogic coach recognises that she is no more 'outside the system' than any other actor in the coachee's world. To engage in dialogue with a coachee is to play a role in the creation of meaning that may have effects well beyond the coaching room.

The dialogic coach is more likely to express curiosity about the past. As David Drake puts it 'While much of coaching is future focussed people often need to re-story the past as part of the process. People draw on their past, present, and future identities in telling their stories'.[12] Drake talks about coaching as the convergence of three selves: the constructed self (from the past), the lived self (in the present) and the imagined self (in the future). Each self is inextricably connected to the other. Dialogue facilitates the surfacing of these different selves, and the emergence of new relationships between these selves, in service of meeting a specific challenge in a particular context.

The traditional coach is likely to be a strong advocate of coaching becoming a classic profession: coaching is about competency and skill, and we need to make sure the unskilled can't call themselves coaches. The dialogic coach is unlikely to be so interested in becoming a professional: it's hard to depict the capacity to engage in dialogue in terms of skills and competencies, but he may nevertheless be interested in what may emerge from the dialogue that takes place around the issue.

Table 2.1

	Traditional	Dialogic	Systemic
Typical area of practice	Dyadic	Dyadic, key stakeholders and group	
Leadership model	Leader as individual	Leadership as relational	
Primary loyalty	To coachee	To coachee and key relationships	
Approach to confidentiality	Maintain strict confidence	Contract boundaries and encourage dialogue	
Role identity	Objective agent, outside system	Subjective co-creator, within relationships	
Listening credo	Listen to understand	Listen to create space for reflection and change	
Attention to goals	Focus on conscious self-regulation	Focus on emergence of intention in the relationship	
Looking forwards and backwards	Focus forwards	Look backwards to understand moving forwards	
View on coach as professional	Advocate	Positive/neutral/oppose	

This is the dialogic approach. What's next?

Notes

1 Emerson, B. & Loehr, A. (2008). *A Manager's Guide to Coaching*. AMACOM: New York.
2 Kahane, A. (2008). *Solving Tough Problems: An Open Way of Talking, Listening and Creating New Realities*, 2nd edition. Berrett-Koehler: San Francisco, CA.
3 Isaacs, W (1999). *Dialogue and the Art of Thinking Together*. Currency Doubleday: New York.
4 Reinhard Stelter is a passionate advocate of dialogue. He defines 'third generational' coaching as a form of coaching in which there is 'genuine' dialogue between coach and coachee. See [Stelter, R. (2012). *A Guide to Third Generation Coaching*. Springer: Heidelberg.]
5 Again, lots of references. For example, Price and van Dick's introduction to a special issue of the *Journal of Change Management* on change and identity [Price, D. & van Dick, R. (2012). Identity and change: Recent developments and future directions. *Journal of Change Management*, 12(1), 7–11] and in a coaching context [Drake, D.B. (2015). *Narrative Coaching*, CNC: Petaluma, CA].
6 Moore, A. & Rybeck, J. (2015). *Coaching for the 21st century*. Korn Ferry Institute whitepaper. www.kornferry.com/institute/coaching-21st-century.
7 For example, [Kets de Vries, M. (2006). *The Leader on the Couch*. Jossey-Bass: San Francisco, CA].
8 Drake, D.B. (2015). *Narrative Coaching*. CNC: Petaluma, CA.
9 Ibarra, H. (2013). Foreword to: David, S., Clutterbuck, D. & Megginson, D. *Beyond Goals*. Gower: Surrey.
10 Locke, E.A. & Latham, G.P. (1990). *A Theory of Goal Setting and Task Performance*. Prentice-Hall: Englewood Cliffs, NJ.
11 Clutterbuck, D. (2010). Coaching Reflection: The Liberated Coach. *Coaching: An International Journal of Theory, Research and Practice*, 3(1), 73–81.
12 Drake, D.B. (2015). *Narrative Coaching*. CNC: Petaluma, CA.

3

The Systemic Approach

In Chapter 2 we said the dialogic approach is different to the traditional approach, in that it's based on a belief that change emerges from interactions between people. The role of the dialogic coach is to create a space in which change is most likely to emerge.

All coaches engage in conversation. The dialogic coach is constantly attuned to the difference between dialogue and other forms of conversation.

The systemic approach is a progression of the dialogic approach. The systemic coach understands that change emerges from a broad pattern of dialogue. Not all interactions in the system are local or easily visible; but the impact of those interactions may nevertheless ripple through the system without obvious cause and effect.[1] The systemic coach is alert to these ripples, to the impact of events outside the coachee's immediate environment that may nevertheless be impacting upon that environment. A little later in this chapter we'll provide a concrete example of the difference between the systemic approach and other approaches. First though we need to spend a little time on change theory.

Change theory

Traditional approaches to change are as questionable as traditional approaches to coaching. There exist at least two quite different approaches to change. Most decision makers inside organisations still cling to the old approach to change, an approach that doesn't look good when we start thinking about complexity. The traditional approach to change goes something like this:

1 Gather lots of data.
2 Work out what the issue is.
3 Decide on a solution.
4 Tell everyone in the organisation what they need to do differently.
5 Make sure they do it.
6 When people do what they're supposed to do – congratulate them in public.
7 Keep going until the change is 'embedded'.

The primary skill of an effective change manager, in this scenario, is planning. People like this approach to change. They like it because it implies that change can be directed and controlled. It implies that the only real obstacles to change are our own capacities to communicate, direct and organise – all good leadership attributes we can design workshops for. However, there are some implicit assumptions in this approach that are problematic. For example, it assumes that the 'change' in question can be decided upon by a few people. All you need is data. The change is decided upon and the task of the change advocate is to explain the importance of the change to others (usually) further down the organisation. This is a perspective that privileges the role of hierarchy and positional power. The mandate for change is communicated to the rest of the organisation, who are expected to comply. If the organisation is slow to respond, then the message is repeated. Often it takes several attempts at communicating the message before anything happens. Traditional change theorists recognise this and encourage leaders to keep going. For example:

> Communications must be a priority for every manager at every level of the company. It is important for the messages to be consistent, clear, and endlessly repeated. If there is a single rule of communication for leaders, it is this: when you are so sick of talking about something that you can hardly stand it, your message is finally starting to get through.[2]

Notice how the word 'communication' is being used in a monologic sense here, with the emphasis on telling. The word 'communication' can also be used in a dialogic sense, with equal emphasis on listening and telling, but that's not how it's often used by change theorists. Laurie Lewis and colleagues explored this in 2006.[3] They obtained copies of the 100 bestselling books on organisational change as listed by Amazon.com and analysed those books to identify what were the most common pieces of advice. Most texts emphasised the importance of communication. Often this was directive 'communication', occasionally it was more participative. Four books even advocated the use of threats or punishment if people failed to comply with the change message, including one that included a section entitled 'Enlist star power or have a public hanging'.

Some authors advocate consultation in service of alignment; workshops and meetings for example, but not with an intent to listen or foster dialogue. Often the fundamental purpose for change is already decided. The wonderful word 'facipulation' has emerged to describe situations in which the espoused purpose is to consult, whereas the actual purpose is to attain compliance. The explicit message is 'Let's agree together'. The implicit message is 'This is what we have decided. Please do your bit in making sure it gets done'.[4] This is a 'them and us' approach to change. We are the people who have all the data that points overwhelmingly to the need for a certain course of action. They are the people who refuse to buy in, despite our indisputable compelling logic. They are 'resistant to change'.

Any approach that starts with just a few people at the top of an organisation working out what needs to happen, then proceeds through a series of linear steps to effectively persuade the rest of the organisation to get on board, is necessarily monologic. The systemic approach to change recognises that the world is complex and ever-changing, that there exist multiple perspectives of the here-and-now that will only ever be partially represented by available data. From this perspective 'resistance to change' is quite natural. Resistance, expressed skilfully or otherwise, may be usefully interpreted as the asking of a question.[5]

There exists a different perspective on change, not a particularly new perspective, but one that organisations continue to show little interest in – perhaps because it challenges the notion that change can be controlled. It questions the pre-eminence of positional power. It paints a picture of a world that is inherently ambiguous, volatile and unpredictable. The basic premise of this alternative perspective on change is:

1   Different people sit in different places and see the world differently. All these perspectives are valid.
2   People won't be told what to think.
3   People decide what to think by talking to people they trust.
4   People talk to lots of other people.
5   You can't predict who people will talk to. People talk to other people at the café, the gym, social events, etc.
6   People tend to do what they think is right, unless someone stands over them with a big stick.
7   Change emerges from the relationships between lots of different people. This process is unpredictable and cannot be controlled.

A couple of years ago, we interviewed 50 leaders across the world, asking them how they had successfully led change.[6] We found one person who recommended the first approach. She was brought in to change the culture of an organisation that had been caught out by external regulators. Staff had flouted the rules in service of making large sums of money. The regulators were threatening to close the business unless changes were made fast. This leader took the view that the required changes would be impossible to implement without miscreant staff being asked to leave. She consulted with her board to work out what changes needed to be made, then set about implementing them. Anyone who didn't comply was asked to leave. Lots of people were asked to leave, and the organisation went through a period of misery and poor performance. But the business survived.

The other 49 leaders described the second approach. They worked outside the parameters of the organisation chart and made a point of getting to know people across and outside their organisations. They listened to what others had to say and shared their own opinions, without fear of being contradicted. From those conversations emerged a clear direction. Sometimes the new direction wasn't very different to the direction the leaders were thinking of at the start. Occasionally it was very different. Most often it was just a bit different, but in all cases the new direction reflected the collective perspective of the organisation, which then went about change without needing to be prodded and cajoled.

An example. I work in the branch of a bank with my ten colleagues. One day we are informed that we must start trying to 'on-sell'. If someone comes into the branch asking for a loan, we must offer them life insurance as well. It is explained that this approach will increase sales – the data is indisputable. It appears we are expected to comply immediately with this edict. Instead I talk to my colleagues and share with them my concerns. Most of our customers have been coming to us for years. They will hate this 'on-selling' strategy. They already make jokes about what it's like going to the local fast-food restaurant ('do you want fries with that?') or to the cinema ('would you like a drink with your popcorn?'). If we start doing it too it'll be like we're betraying our customers! All my colleagues agree, and so we ring up our district manager and tell him 'This won't work! Our customers will hate it!'

It doesn't sound like a question, does it? But it is. It's a question phrased in such a way as to make sure you listen, because we don't have a lot of confidence that you *will* listen. The question is, 'how do we implement this new on-selling strategy without upsetting our longstanding customers, potentially losing their business?' It is, in effect, an invitation to engage in dialogue. The response to such a question however, is usually to repeat the original message and insist upon compliance – more monologue.

So what?

So, meaning making is social. In this case the management of the bank *told* its employees to change the way they behaved. They provided a rationale that they assumed made sense. However, they relied too heavily on data, data that says 'on-selling increases sales'. They failed to explore their new idea with people in the organisation who had a different perspective, a perspective based on spending their entire working day talking to customers. Yet they still expected the new strategy to be implemented. They failed to recognise that this isn't how change works. Change is constant – like it or not – and change emerges from the interactions between people. Not everyone is compliant. People make sense of events for themselves through conversation with others. They will do this whether or not they are asked to. The wise change advocate recognises the uncomfortable truth, that positional power is not absolute and that change emerges from dialogue. The wise change advocate seeks every opportunity to engage in that dialogue. In this case, senior executives from the bank have a change of heart and decide to visit our branch to engage in open dialogue. They listen without prejudice, suspending their deeply held beliefs in what the data is telling them, and begin to understand our perspective. We feel heard, and from that dialogue emerges something new and different, to which everyone is committed.

Systemic ≠ systematic

These two words have fundamentally different meanings, yet they get used interchangeably, particularly when talking about 'systems thinking'. The **systematic** perspective recognises that the world is extremely complicated, that you can't jump to conclusions, that the obvious answer may be the wrong answer. Nevertheless the 'systematic' thinker does believe that if you analyse long enough you will find a predictable order and logic. The 'systematic' perspective is logical and rational. The world is like an aircraft engine; hard to understand on first inspection, but ultimately comprehensible. The **systemic** perspective acknowledges the existence of order, but is based on a belief that this order is not only hard to fathom, but it is constantly changing. Systems exist within systems within systems within systems, and every component of the system is constantly interacting with other components. This is the world of wind systems and ocean currents. You may gain glimpses of great clarity and discern broad patterns, but as soon as you think you have a grasp on what's happening, then the system has changed again. You too, are a component of the system. You influence its functioning, but you cannot control it.

Implications for the leader

In this systemic theory of change, dialogue plays a central role. Dialogue is the medium of interaction and so change emerges from dialogue. Therefore, if I want to *guide* change in my organisation, recognising that I cannot *direct* it, then I must work out with whom I need to engage in dialogue, about what, and when. The systemic approach is about looking out for patterns of conversation and working out how we can most effectively participate in those conversations. It's about spotting which conversations need to be dialogic, and intervening accordingly. This has big implications for how leaders lead. Consider this quote by Margaret Wheatley:[7]

Here is a very partial list of new metaphors to describe leaders: gardeners, midwives, stewards, servants, missionaries, facilitators, conveners. Although each takes a slightly different approach, they all name a new posture for leaders, a stance that relies on new relationships with their networks of employees, stakeholders, and communities. No one can hope to lead any organization by standing outside or ignoring the web of relationships through which all work is accomplished.

This frame on leadership is systemic. It goes beyond a realisation that relationships are 'important'. Uhl-Bien and colleagues[8] write: 'Complexity science suggests a different paradigm for leadership – one that frames leadership as a complex interactive dynamic from which adaptive outcomes (e.g., learning, innovation, and adaptability) emerge'.

In traditional leadership theory, the unit of analysis is the individual leader. Through the systemic lens the fundamental unit of analysis is the complex adaptive system[9]. Systemic leaders are more likely to see themselves as 'gardeners, midwives, stewards, facilitators, conveners' of the system. They are more likely to be focused on relationships and networks, and how best to engage. As Conklin puts it:[10]

In the emerging paradigm, something new is happening. In place of prediction and control, we seem to have nothing but chaos; in place of individual efforts, the problem-solving process is now clearly social; in place of basing decisions on facts, we base them on stories that give us more coherent sense of meaning. In place of finding the 'right' answer, we seek to gain a shared understanding of possible solutions.

This view of leadership is intrinsically relational. Leadership becomes something we do together rather than an individual attribute. Leadership becomes a dynamic, fluid process through which organisations make meaning of current events and move together. The 'technology' through which this all happens is dialogue.

I'm a coach. What does all this have to do with me?

If this is how change works, and if this is what leadership is all about, then the traditional approach to coaching won't always be effective. If my coachee tells me she wants to be more influential, what do I get curious about? From a traditional perspective, I probably get curious about my coachee's skill levels. How good is she at listening to other people's points of view? How good is she at presenting a compelling case? These may be useful conversations to have, they may not. It may be more useful for my coachee to get curious about the way the organisation works. Who talks to who? Where does dialogue take place and where does it not? Who do I want to engage in dialogue with; about what?

Consider too the idea that our identities are subject to dialogue. Our lives are full of different people with different needs.[11] We respond to each of these people differently. To the poor-performing direct report with no apparent motivation to improve, I may show up as 'authoritative me'. To my passionate peer, full of new ideas, some good some not so good, I may show up as 'rational me'. To my procrastinating boss, I may show up as 'decisive me'. We each have multiple identities, identities that are constantly evolving through our ongoing interactions with others.

I am coaching Rob. We had a good session last month and he left the session apparently resolved as to who he was going to be as leader to his team ('energetic direction setter'), who he was going to be as peer ('sympathetic ear'), and who he was going to be as direct report to his line manager ('dependable deliverer'). We met again yesterday. The company had a tough month and he's had lots of deep and meaningful conversations. As we talk so I can discern that each of these identities has shifted and changed. To make sense of these changes I must develop a sense of the system, the pattern of relationships, within which Rob is operating.

This focus on patterns will inevitably create a picture of the organisation in the coach's mind. We're not talking here about the organisation chart, a copy of which we may already have been given by the client. The organisation chart is interesting, but it provides only one lens on the way the company operates; the hierarchy, the 'positional power map'. Few organisations are energised solely through positional power. The systemic coach looks for patterns of dialogue and relates to the organisation as a story, a story that is constantly being told and retold, interpreted and re-interpreted, through multiple frames of reference. The systemic coach seeks to understand the coachee's interpretation of the organisational story, and to locate his/her own role within that system.

Systemic coaching in practice

In Chapters 1 and 2 we looked at transcripts of conversations between Adam and Jill. It's hard to represent systemic coaching in the same way because the coach's behaviour constantly reflects the awareness he/she has of being part of the bigger system. Systemic coaching may be best illustrated by telling the story at a distance.

In our scenario, you may recall, Adam thinks he needs to be more influential. His manager told him he should go to Toastmasters and his colleague in HR told him he needs to build more of a presence among the senior executive. Adam is puzzled because this didn't happen in the last organisation he worked at. There he had good relationships with the senior executive team with whom he interacted regularly at steering committee meetings. Everyone said he was clear and articulate, presented a good argument and received feedback well. Yes, he needs to find himself amidst the chaos of this new role, but still he's puzzled – what's changed?

Jill suggests it would be helpful if she could witness Adam in conversation with key stakeholders. She suggests the two of them meet with George, Adam's manager, to get his input into the 'goal-setting process'. George agrees, and so the three of them meet one afternoon in a small meeting room with three chairs and a round table. The meeting starts well enough, with Adam outlining the business context as he sees it and his struggles to get everything done. George appears sympathetic, but draws the line at stopping any of the projects or shifting timelines. Jill notices how uncomfortable George becomes at any suggestion that a project be deferred. His mantra, which he repeats several times, is 'We just have to find a way'. George takes every opportunity to shift the conversation away from postponing projects, to Adam's behaviour at the executive table. He wants Adam to speak up more, to request more resources from other departments, to make a compelling case for all the projects he has been asked to lead.

Jill becomes curious as to the relationship between George and *his* boss, the CEO, and between George and his peers. George is relatively new to the organisation and seems anxious to make a good impression. He seems unwilling to push back, committed to building a reputation for getting things done. George cuts short the meeting with Jill and Adam on the basis that he is very busy. After the meeting, Jill and Adam share their experiences of the conversation and they reflect on George's reluctance to talk about his relationship with the CEO. At the end of the conversation Adam commits to taking every opportunity he can to watch George in action with the CEO and the rest of the executive team.

Jill and Adam meet again five weeks later. Adam has attended four meetings with George and the CEO, at two of which the Chief Financial Officer (CFO) was also present Adam reports back that the CEO and George get on well when they are left alone, but the dynamic changes when the CFO enters the room. The CFO is a big man, hale and hearty. He has a clear vision for the company and holds strong views. The CFO is constantly challenging the CEO and takes great delight in catching him out on any aspect of the organisation with which he is unfamiliar. He looks to

George to back him up, making eye contact with George and saying things like 'isn't that right, George?' and 'Wouldn't you say, George?' The CFO is usually right, but the points he makes aren't important. Nor, in George's view, should the CEO be expected to understand every little detail of the company's operation. However, the one time George tried to express this view he got slapped down by the CEO apparently embarrassed at the possibility George thought he needed protecting. The CFO just smiled quietly and continued to prompt George to back him up. At both meetings, the CEO became terse and critical, venting his frustrations on George. George left both meetings in a bad temper and vented his frustrations on Adam, making it clear both times that he had no intention of revisiting the actions he had agreed, with either the CEO or the CFO. What was agreed to just had to get done – 'we just have to find a way . . .'

Accessing this systemic view as to how the organisation was functioning, including Adam's role in that system, enabled both Jill and Adam to see that little was likely to be resolved by Adam attending Toastmasters or attempting to prioritise more effectively or seeking to postpone the eighth project. Yes, Adam would have to manage a tendency to try and keep everyone happy, but the systemic analysis offered up more useful insights besides. After a long conversation, Adam committed to doing some work with senior managers in the CFO's department, helping them to see the benefit of focusing on landing a few projects well. And he committed to finding out which of the eight projects the CEO was most interested in. This would allow Adam to approach his line manager from a fresh angle, giving him the assurance he required to agree to defer a couple of projects. Adam didn't go to Toastmasters but he did end up feeling more confident about his abilities to get things done *in this system*.

Three approaches compared

In Chapter 2 we contrasted the traditional approach to the dialogic approach. The traditional coach is focused on good communication, making sure he understands the coachee, in service of helping the coachee to work out what he wants to do next. Listening and effective voicing are important to the dialogic coach because this form of conversation generates change. The dialogic coach recognises her role in the relationship, as co-creator of whatever change emerges. The systemic coach recognises that dialogue sits at the heart of individual, team and organisational change. To understand an issue requires understanding patterns of conversation and the presence/absence of dialogue in those interactions (Figure 3.1). Change is social and systemic.

In what other ways can we tell the difference between the three approaches? Take Table 3.1 with a pinch of salt since it attempts to categorise each approach firmly into one of three buckets. The reality is that coaches have a multitude of different practice models, many of which are quite eclectic. Nevertheless, the comparison may be of some use in identifying a dominant approach.

If my dominant approach is **traditional**, then I am likely to spend most of my time coaching individuals. Adhering to a credo that says you can change the leadership of an organisation leader by leader, I see the work that I do makes a direct contribution to the efficacy of the organisation. I see myself as an outsider to the organisation, a non-participant whose

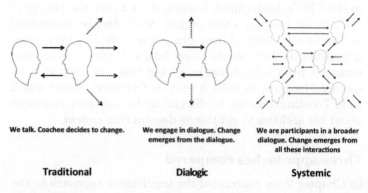

We talk. Coachee decides to change.   We engage in dialogue. Change emerges from the dialogue.   We are participants in a broader dialogue. Change emerges from all these interactions

Traditional   **Dialogic**   **Systemic**

Figure 3.1

role it is to facilitate change in individuals. I readily identify with established coaching competencies and coaching ethics, and believe coaching conversations should be future focused, with minimal time spent reflecting on the past. All sessions should end with a commitment to specific actions. There is no need for me to seek out conversations with others in the organisation other than to make sure goals are initially aligned. When push comes to shove, I prioritise the needs of my coachees and will do whatever I can to make sure what gets said in the coaching room, stays in the coaching room.

If my dominant approach is **dialogic,** I see my role differently. My role isn't only about listening to understand but also to create a space from which may emerge new insights that neither I nor the coachee initially brought into the room. I am part of the system, and I play an integral role in the co-creative process. I pay attention to my coachee's narration of the past as a means of understanding their narration of the present. I understand that meaning and identity are both constructed in the relationship, and that through the interaction the coachee can construct new meanings and new identities. I recognise that goals change and evolve and that for all parties to remain aligned as to the purpose of coaching, dialogue needs to happen. I have a role to play in ensuring that dialogue takes place, and fulfilling that role most effectively may require me to talk to people outside the coaching room about what is happening inside the coaching room. Confidentiality is of course important, but I talk more about the importance of contracting. I also coach groups, but don't yet feel fully prepared to move into team coaching, where an understanding of 'process' may be required: the ability to identify and work with patterns of dialogue.

If my dominant approach is **systemic**, I also see the world through a dialogic lens. Change emerges from dialogue. I don't experience an individual coaching assignment as a relationship between two people. The rest of the organisational system is ever present, playing a role in whatever is said in the room. Both the coachee and I are part of that

Table 3.1

	Traditional	Dialogic	Systemic
Typical area of practice	Dyadic	Dyadic, key stakeholders and group	Dyadic, group, team, organisation, world
Leadership model	Leader as individual	Leadership as relational	Leadership as relational & systemic
Primary loyalty	To coachee	To coachee and key relationships	To the broader system
Approach to confidentiality	Maintain strict confidence	Contract boundaries and encourage dialogue	Contract boundaries and encourage dialogue
Role identity	Objective agent, outside system	Subjective co-creator, within relationships	Subjective co-creator, within relationships, within system
Listening credo	Listen to understand	Listen to create space for reflection and change	Listen for patterns of dialogue and story, to create space for organisational change
Attention to goals	Focus on conscious self-regulation	Focus on emergence of intention in the relationship	Focus on emergence of intention in the system
Looking forwards and backwards	Focus forwards	Look backwards to understand in service of moving forwards	Look backwards to understand cultural, organisational, team and individual identities in service of moving forwards
View on coach as professional	Advocate	Positive/neutral/oppose	Debate on professionalism seen as an event in the coaching industry's evolution as a complex dynamic system

system, both influencing and being influenced by people outside the room, albeit sometimes indirectly. If asked to whom, if pressed, I am most loyal, coachee or organisation, I will likely take a while to answer. How can I interact with the coachee without interacting with the system? And how is it useful to the coachee for me to choose not to interact directly with other people in that system? The question holds no meaning; I am most loyal to the system. Just as the dialogic coach will seek to understand better the identity of the coachee by exploring the formation of that identity in the past, so I will be just as interested in the identity and culture of the organisation and how that has evolved over time. I am neutral as to arguments around profession-alisation. For me the fact that the industry is engaged in such conversation just *is*. The coaching community, like any other sizeable, international, dispersed community, is complex. People will talk and make sense of themselves as a community of practitioners with reference to existing mental models. This dialogue will continue and change will emerge, quite probably in a direction no one yet envisages.

Notes

1 O'Connor, S. & Cavanagh, M. (2013). The coaching ripple effect: The effects of developmental coaching on wellbeing across organisational networks. *Psychology of Well-Being: Theory, Research and Practice*, 3(1), 2.
2 Duck, J.D. (1998). Managing change: the art of balancing. *Harvard Business Review*, 71 (6), 109–118.
3 Lewis, L.K., Schmisseir, A.M., Stephens, K. & Weir, K.E. (2006). Advice on communicating during organizational change. *Journal of Business Communication*, 43 (2), 113–137.
4 Jabri, M., Adrian, A.D. & Boje, D. (2008). Reconsidering the role of conversations in change communication: a contribution based on Bakhtin. *Journal of Organizational Change Management*, 21 (6), 667–685.
5 Ford, J.D. & Ford, L.W. (2010) Stop blaming resistance to change and start using it. *Organizational Dynamics*, 39 (1), 24–36.
6 The results of the study were reported in both a book [Lawrence, P. (2014). *Leading Change. How Successful Leaders Approach Change Management*. Kogan Page: London] and an article

[Lawrence, P. (2015). Leading change – Insights into how leaders actually approach the challenge of complexity. *Journal of Change Management* 15(3), 231–252].

7   Wheatley, M.J. (2006). *Leadership and the New Science: Discovering Order in a Chaotic World*. Berrett-Koehler: San Francisco, CA.

8   Uhl-Bien, M., Marion, R. & McKelvey, B. (2007). Complexity Leadership Theory: Shifting leadership from the industrial age to the knowledge era. *The Leadership Quarterly*, 18(4), 298–318.

9   Moore, A. (2014). *Practices of Relational Leadership in Action Learning Teams*. Tilburg University: Tilburg.

10 Conklin, J. (2009). Building shared understanding of wicked problems. *Rotman Magazine*, Winter, 16–20.

11 A point made by several of the contributors to [Holman, D.J. & Thorpe, R. (2003). *Management & Language*. SAGE: London]. Especially the chapter by Holman, D.J, Gold, J. & Thorpe, R.: Full of characters: identity and talk in practical authoring.

Coaching PRACTICE

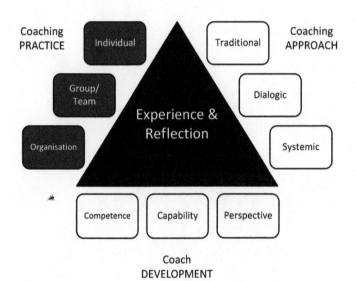

Coaching PRACTICE

Individual

Group/Team

Organisation

Experience & Reflection

Traditional

Coaching APPROACH

Dialogic

Systemic

Competence

Capability

Perspective

Coach DEVELOPMENT

Some coaches work exclusively with **individuals**, some with **teams/groups** and others work at a broader level with their clients, helping them to think through how to design and implement interventions at the **organisational** level. We'll explore in this section the interplay between **approach** and **practice** illustrating, for example, some practical ways in which a systemic coach might go about working with individuals. We'll look at some of the commonalities and differences between the different areas of practice and how differences in approach may help coaches transition from one area of practice to another.

Some coaches work exclusively with **individuals**, some with teams/groups and others work at a broader level with their clients, helping them to think through how to design and implement interventions at the organisational level. We'll explore in this section the interplay between **approach** and **practice**, illustrating, for example, some practical ways in which a coach to the coach might go about working with individuals. We'll look at some of the commonalities and differences between the different areas of practice and how differences in approach may help coaches transition from one area of practice to another.

4

A Systemic Approach to Coaching Individuals

In Chapters 1 and 2 we illustrated what traditional and dialogic coaching might look like in practice. We refrained from providing a similar transcript for systemic coaching and presented instead a mini-case study. We imagine that many readers will be looking for us to provide a more in-depth account as to what systemic coaching might look like, a need we shall attempt to address in this chapter.

It's hard to be prescriptive as to what systemic coaching looks like, not least because we all have parameters to work within. A client might be really interested in working with us because we say we work systemically, but may not have a budget for us to do much work outside the coaching room, or the client may work in an organisation where other stakeholders are reluctant to directly participate in someone else's coaching assignment. From a systemic perspective, we can't anyway walk into such scenarios with a prescribed approach. If we are coming to an assignment with the intention of engaging in dialogue (rather than monologue) we come ready for solutions to emerge. We can nevertheless identify three aspects of systemic practice that may be helpful:

1 Inviting the system into the room
2 Encouraging feedback
3 Collaborating

Inviting the system into the room

By bringing the system into the room we co-create an environment in which coachees can reflect upon themselves within the context of a broader set of interactions. There are two ways to achieve this. First, you can invite coachees to bring their perspective on the system into the dialogue. Second, you can directly invite other components of the system into the room.

Talking about the system – Bob

Bob headed up a clinical service in a hospital in the USA. The hospital was managed by a health organisation that managed two hospitals in the same city. Bob was asked by general management to work with the other service director, to come up with a best-in-class process to be implemented across both hospitals. Bob was chosen to lead the project because of ground-breaking work he had led in his own unit. It was widely expected that Bob and Lorna (his counterpart) would work closely together in coming up with new processes to be rolled out across both locations. To implement Bob's new process in the other unit would mean recruiting people with new skills and redeploying people with skills that were no longer required.

Bob and Lorna got off to a difficult start. From Bob's perspective, she had a strong emotional resistance to making staff changes. He found her hard to get hold of and slow to deliver on her commitments. Bob handled the relationship as diplomatically as he could and avoided getting into an argument. As the study progressed, staff in both hospitals became increasingly enthusiastic about the proposed changes, and keen to get going. At the end of the study Bob wrote a draft report and sent it to Lorna to review. However, Lorna went on extended leave without responding. Bob submitted his recommendations anyway, up to his manager. His manager said she would need to get the CEO's approval before being able to approve the report.

Bob showed up to coaching worried. Two months on and he still hadn't heard back. He reminded his manager twice of the need to decide, but on both occasions, she told him he would have to wait; the CEO was engaged in more urgent matters. In a hierarchical and bureaucratic organisation, Bob didn't want to go direct to the CEO, for fear of angering his line manager. In the meantime, he heard his reputation being questioned. People were saying things like 'Bob's leading the project and nothing's happened. Bob has no influence.' Bob also heard that the resident clinician at the other hospital was angry with him for holding back on the new process. Bob didn't know the clinician very well, but he was indeed loath to proceed with the new process without first skilling people up to implement it. Implementing the process without putting the right people in place would lead to failure.

Bob felt stuck. He talked about feeling powerless, unable to do much about his 'sinking reputation'. His line manager was unresponsive and the whole project seemed stuck in a bottleneck. As the dialogue unfolded so Bob became aware of some of the mental models that guided his thinking. They included:

- A tendency to criticise himself and question his own decisions
- A dislike of confrontation
- Privileging the role of positional power in the organisation

Bob drew a diagram of the key relationships in the organisation. The drawing reflects the importance of hierarchy in his own mental model (Figure 4.1). It's from this perspective that Bob felt powerless, unable to see how he could influence effectively up the line.

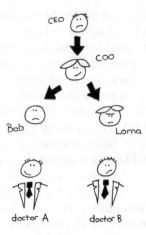

Figure 4.1

As he talked more about relationships within the system he started to categorise each of them as 'strong', 'weak' and 'adversarial'. New insights emerged:

- The two clinicians (one in each hospital) had considerable 'expert' power. Neither were employees, yet both were regarded as indispensable. If they withdrew their services, then neither unit would be able to operate and there were few other clinicians with their expertise available.
- Bob also had 'expert' power. He was well known in the global research community and his presence at the hospital made it relatively easy for the hospital to obtain research funds in his area.
- Bob also had considerable 'network' power. He had harmonious relationships with his line manager and the CEO, who both held him in high esteem. He got on well with the clinician at his hospital. The only person he didn't have a good relationship with was Lorna. He hadn't met Doctor B.

- Lorna didn't have great 'network' power. She didn't get on particularly well with their line manager and didn't have much of a relationship at all with the CEO or the clinician at her hospital.
- The two clinicians got on like a house on fire. They respected each other's expertise and engaged in regular dialogue. Neither of them much liked Bob's line manager or the CEO.

As Bob considered his dilemma, he amended the diagram (Figure 4.2):

As Bob stared at the sketch he noticed he had drawn himself near the bottom of the page, consistent with his focus on positional power. He had drawn the two clinicians low down too, since neither of them had a role in the official hierarchy. Yet much of the power in the system sat with the three of them. The solution to his dilemma became clear. He would talk to doctor A and seek an introduction to doctor B. He

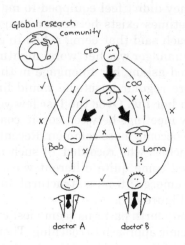

Figure 4.2

would ask to meet with both to initiate a dialogue around the project. Both clinicians agreed and between them they agreed a plan of action. The key action item was that the clinicians would make a formal request to the CEO to action recommendations from the report. About a week later Bob finally heard from his line manager that the project was approved.

Inviting others into the dialogue – three-way meetings

A couple of years ago, we interviewed 33 organisational coaches seeking to understand their views on supervision.[1] Only 12% said they used supervision to discuss the challenges of engaging with other stakeholders in the organisation or otherwise addressing the complexity of the system. Many said that they weren't asked to engage with other stakeholders in the system, such that it wasn't an issue. Many who were asked to engage with line managers, for example, sought to get the conversation over as quickly as possible. They didn't feel equipped to manage the tension that sometimes exists between manager and direct report. One coach said that being asked to engage with a coachee's line manager was her 'worst nightmare' and that if people started asking her to engage in those conversations on a more regular basis she would find something else to do with her life. Over the last few years we sense that three-way meetings between coach, coachee and line manager have become more common. Recently we worked with seven coaches, who recorded 14 such meetings. The results revealed some quite different ways of operating. Four patterns emerged from a structural analysis of each conversation (Figure 4.3).

The third and fourth patterns seem most consistent with a dialogic/systemic approach to coaching. Though the stated purpose of each of these meetings was to encourage the line manager to contribute to goal setting, a minority of coaches steered the conversation toward three other areas besides:

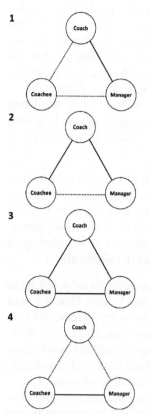

1 The coach directed most questions at the line manager, seeking to elicit the line manager's input into goal setting.

2 The coach sought to get both coachee and line manager's input into the conversation by asking them the same questions in turn. Within this structure line manager and coachee spoke little directly to each other.

3 Coach, coachee and line manager all contributed to the conversation in roughly equal proportions. Sometimes this happened because everyone was determined to speak, sometimes it happened because the coach was clearly working hard to encourage coachee and line manager to talk to each other.

4 The coach introduced the purpose of the meeting then sat back to allow coachee and line manager to interact directly from the start.

Figure 4.3

1 One coach explicitly raised the issue as to how the line manager could support the coachee in their efforts to change a behaviour. Coach, coachee and line manager then had a conversation in which coachee and line manager contracted around which of these roles the line manager was prepared to fulfil.

2 One coach invited coachee (Alan) and line manager (Nancy) to reflect on their relationship as it was playing

out in the meeting. Alan had earlier pledged to ask for feedback on his efforts to articulate his point of view clearly and concisely. He acknowledged he hadn't always received feedback well in the past, and Nancy acknowledged that she found it challenging to give him feedback in the moment. Following this exchange Nancy asked Alan about his experience of speaking out in meetings with the senior executive. Alan's response was long and non-specific. Nancy nodded and changed the subject, at which the coach interrupted:

> I'd like to just go back to what was just said. Is that OK? I noticed that when you, Alan, answered Nancy's question, your answer was quite long, and I didn't understand everything you said. Then you, Nancy, nodded and changed the subject. I'm wondering, is this an example of what we were talking about?

The coach then facilitated a conversation between Alan and Nancy in which Alan acknowledged that he had provided a long and rambling answer because he was uncertain how to answer the question, the very behaviour he was seeking to change, and Nancy acknowledged that she had consciously decided not to provide feedback, again a behaviour she had committed to change.

3   Two coaches proactively encouraged coachee and line manager to think about the coachee's intentions in the context of the wider organisational agenda. Inviting the participants to think from multiple perspectives always triggered new insights around navigating key relationships in the organisation.

We should be careful in concluding whether each of the coaches engaged in this study were adopting traditional, dialogic or systemic approaches. Reaching judgement based only on a fragment of a coaching assignment would be risky. Nevertheless, the findings tend to support the idea that many coaches think in traditional terms. Their primary focus seemed to be clarifying individual goals and the development of the individual.

Engaging multiple stakeholders – Helen

An unusual request

Last year we received a phone call. A client we hadn't worked with before asked us to coach someone through a two-day intensive. They didn't want to fund a conventional assignment over an extended period because the CEO wanted to see change happen faster. Our initial thought was to turn the assignment down. It went against all traditional wisdoms as we understood them. How can you coach someone for two days straight? Wouldn't they get tired? And what would happen afterwards? We would have no scope for reflecting with the coachee on how she had gone against her goals. Furthermore, we got the sense that this assignment was the CEO's idea and the 'coaching' agenda was coercive. But we challenged ourselves. If the essence of coaching is dialogue, then there's no reason why results can't be achieved outside a traditional framework. So, we took the next step and asked for more information.

The brief

Helen was a product manager in a retail bank. Both the CEO (Jim) and the OD manager thought her style was abrasive and confrontational. Jim asked the OD manager to find an intervention that would 'fix' Helen quickly because key clients were starting to complain. Also, Helen's staff were grumbling, and her new manager was becoming impatient. Helen's new manager was Shireen, appointed to a role that Helen had applied for unsuccessfully. Helen had nevertheless done well in the assessment centre, showing up as highly effective.

Helen

We met Helen and found her to be friendly and engaging. She said she was happy to participate in the process. She had previously reported directly to Jim with whom she said she enjoyed a good relationship. In their last performance review meeting Jim told her she was doing a good job. He said she needed to tone herself down a bit and that it would be a good idea to do that quickly. As far as Helen was concerned, she was highly regarded, considered to be a potential future CEO. She had recently undertaken a 360 survey and the results hadn't been good (in contrast to the assessment centre results). That was because her new manager had loaded her up with far too much work. Shireen was new to the company, keen to make an impression, and didn't understand what was required to complete all the work she wanted done. Helen was worried about the impact this was having on her team.

The OD manager

We met again with the OD manager to discuss the polarity of these views. The OD manager became anxious, worried that Helen was 'pulling the wool over our eyes'. Helen wasn't currently regarded as future CEO material, she said. Indeed, she would be lucky to hold on to her job. The reason the exercise needed to be conducted in two days was that the CEO was under pressure from Shireen to fire Helen. Once again, we thought about whether we should take on this assignment? From where we were sitting it appeared that both Jim and Shireen were unhappy with Helen's performance but hadn't told her so directly. The OD manager seemed to be the meat in the sandwich, a role she seemed keen to pass on to us. So, we thought about withdrawing.

The approach

On the other hand, from a systemic perspective, this was a story about the absence of dialogue. Both Jim and Shireen seemed reluctant to engage directly with Helen and, if the OD manager was right, nor was Helen engaging effectively with direct reports and colleagues. So, we drafted a proposal. We suggested a three-day intervention, the centrepiece of which would be a series of meetings between the coach, Helen, and selected direct reports, colleagues, Jim and Shireen. Each meeting would be a three-way in which one person would be invited to give feedback to Helen in the presence of the coach. The first day would comprise the coach meeting with each stakeholder, exploring their willingness to participate and providing them with guidance as to how they might provide feedback effectively and safely. The design of the third day would emerge from the first two days.

We shared the proposal with Helen who seemed keen to progress. We explored the extent to which Helen genuinely felt committed to the process and any concerns she might have. Her primary concern was that she would be allowed to meet with Jim and Shireen separately. Otherwise she feared Shireen would hijack the conversation and deny Jim the opportunity to speak. She decided who she wanted to engage in the process and declared herself satisfied. Next, we spoke to Jim and Shireen separately, explaining the rationale for the process and the role that Jim and Shireen would need to play for the intervention to be worthwhile. Both signed off on the process.

Day 1

On the first day, we met with each of the feedback-givers in turn, including Jim and Shireen. Of the seven people we spoke to, six seemed well prepared. Helen had taken the time to invite them personally to take part in the process, explaining what value she hoped to gain. One person seemed less sure, one of Helen's peers.

Day 2

On the second day, we met first with Helen. Helen was 20 minutes late for the 30-minute conversation. When she arrived, she explained she was late because she had received an urgent call from Shireen telling her to drop everything and sort out an urgent issue. We talked to Helen about the day and how she was planning to receive the feedback from the seven people lined up to participate. Then we engaged in a series of 40-minute three-way meetings, one after the other.

Helen behaved impeccably throughout the conversations. She acknowledged every comment made, seeking further clarity when appropriate. The feedback givers visibly relaxed after the few minutes of each conversation and, with one exception, shared with Helen everything they had intended to say. At the end of the day we discussed with Helen not only what individual people had said, but what new insights she now had on the way the system was operating.

A couple of aspects became clear to her. First, Jim and Shireen didn't seem to be on the same page. Shireen said she had seen Helen make big changes already, just in the previous couple of months and that Jim had noticed it too. Jim, on the other hand, said he hadn't noticed much change. What did this tell us about the quality of dialogue between Jim and Shireen? Second, the role that HR were playing in the system became apparent. HR was playing a vocal role in urging Jim to act, based on what appeared to be an isolated interaction between Helen and a relatively junior member of the HR team. The HR partner was concerned that an upcoming leadership programme, designed to advocate the company's new values, would be undermined if Helen didn't change the way she behaved, a programme Helen had been unaware of up until that point.

Reflecting on the second day, Helen committed to take some quick early steps to address some of the feedback she had received. She committed to being present in meetings. She committed to making the time to listen to what others had to say. She committed to delegating more, encouraging her team to take greater ownership. She also committed to think more about the feedback before reconvening with us just a few days later.

Day 3

On the third day, we helped Helen commit to sharing her experience with all those who had given her feedback, and putting in place a process whereby they would continue to give her feedback on an ongoing basis. Helen was energised and enthused. Half way through the day we met again with Jim, the CEO. He came to the meeting looking stressed. He endorsed Helen's plan, but brought up a new issue that had happened just the day before. Helen had turned up late (again) to an important meeting with a key client. Helen listened attentively before sharing her dilemma; that she had specifically been told not to attend the meeting by Shireen.

Then we met Shireen. Shireen also looked annoyed. She also endorsed Helen's plan before raising her voice and criticising Helen for not attending the important client meeting. Shireen denied having told Helen not to attend the meeting and continued to berate her, explaining how embarrassed she felt upon being called by the CEO.

After the meeting with Shireen we reflected on the conversation. Helen shrugged her shoulders and said she didn't know what to do. She saw no other course of action other than to make her case direct to Jim. After talking for a while Helen decided to talk to Jim immediately, but rather than complain about Shireen's behaviour she would seek Jim's advice on how best to manage the relationship. Jim was available. He listened to Helen's story and took her question seriously, He explained to Helen how he experienced Shireen, what was important to her and what he had learned about her through the interview process in taking references from old work colleagues. As Jim spoke it became apparent to both Helen and her coach that there existed another side to Shireen that Helen wasn't aware of.

In wrapping up the final day Helen re-committed to her action plan, and reflected upon the system in which she was operating. She reflected on Shireen's background and experience, her preferred way of doing things. She reflected on the nature of the relationship between Jim and Shireen and how she could successfully navigate that. She reflected on the role that HR were playing and some of the relationships she needed to cultivate in order to manage that component of the system effectively. And she reflected on how important it was to build a network of folks across the organisation upon whom she could rely for timely candid feedback on how she was impacting others.

Reflections

Some of you reading this may baulk at this approach. If your approach is more traditional this may not resonate with your own practice model at all. Is this coaching – or is this mediation? Or is it facilitation? Or some form of consultation? Whatever your view, consider the different outcomes of what we are calling a systemic approach to the more traditional approach. Had we in this instance focused our time and energies purely on the individual relationship, then it's possible we would have ended up with some similar actions around listening and delegation. It's less likely that Helen would have truly understood the predicament in which she appeared to find herself. She may have continued to frame the coaching agenda as 'smoothing a few rough edges'. Instead, with the focus on systems and dialogue, Helen became deeply aware as to how she was perceived by others and the consequences of that behaviour. She cultivated new feedback channels that she could continue to leverage. And she gained a whole new perspective on the way the organisation around her was operating vs. the way she believed it should be operating.

This is just an example of a systemic approach to involving multiple stakeholders. We don't offer it as a prescriptive process. This kind of approach might fail disastrously in another context with different players. We offer it as an example of what can emerge when coaches take a dialogic approach to exploring the systems within which they are invited to operate.

Encouraging feedback

Helen's story is a good illustration of a second aspect of good practice: creating feedback loops. Dialogic feedback loops provide rich insights about the self in relation to the system[2]. The traditional approach to change positions change as episodic, small hives of activity taking place against a backdrop of constancy and stability. If this was the way the world operated then it might be sufficient to collect feedback periodically – every six months for example. However, if we believe that the world is more complex, then we recognise that what makes sense on Monday may not make sense by Tuesday. The way I am perceived is personal and contextual. I am likely in relationship with lots of different people, in an ever-changing series of multiple contexts. Collecting feedback on a formal basis, every six to twelve months, may provide useful data, but effective leaders also builds networks of informal feedback channels through which they have access to ongoing real-time feedback.

Remember Adam's quandary? In his previous organisation, he was regarded as articulate and competent. In his new organisation both HR and his line manager tell him he needs to be more influential. Upon investigation, this feedback is obviously highly contextualised. His line manager tells him to assert himself more, because he wants him to get the job done, so he can avoid having difficult conversations with the CEO. If Adam's line manager were to leave his role and be replaced by another manager then no doubt that line manager would have a different perspective. To understand the system, and to be more able to successfully navigate that system, people in that system need access to ongoing feedback as to how they are experienced by multiple specific individuals. This isn't easy to set up. Most of us are wary about giving feedback. Some people ask for feedback when they are asking for assurance. If you're after a pat on the back, even expertly delivered feedback can feel like a kick in the guts. It's hard to answer really open feedback questions. How do you respond to a question like 'Could I have done anything differently?' without knowing what the other person wants to know? It's a lazy question that will often be met with quite a lazy answer 'No – all good.' So, great leaders set an example, not only in receiving feedback well. but in delivering feedback, respectfully and honestly. Building feedback into the system is i) important, ii) hard to do. Helping the coachee to understand the value of an open exchange, and helping the coachee to create new possibilities for exchange within the organisational system, is one of the most valuable contributions a systemic coach can make.

Collaborating

The systemic coach is very aware that when working on an individual coaching assignment, the lens through which he is experiencing the organisational system is narrow. There is a lot going on in the system that the coach can't see. The traditional coach may be loath to spend too much time with the client sponsor or with other coaches, for fear of being asked too many questions. The systemic coach is keen to engage in dialogue with others, having contracted explicitly with his coachees as to what he may or may not divulge. She is keen to engage in such dialogue, because he knows new insights will emerge, useful for everyone involved. The systemic coach welcomes the opportunity to talk to the client sponsor, to access another's perspective on what's happening in the organisation. This is the coachee's world, the system he is seeking to shape and is being shaped by. The systemic coach looks forward to engaging with other coaches working in the same organisation. Each coach will have a different perspective, based not only on their different lenses, but also their unique insight into the functioning of the system.

We have worked on several assignments in which three coaches worked simultaneously with an individual coachee. One coach focuses on the individual, helping the coachee think through their unique traits, values, and sense of purpose. A second coach focuses on the interpersonal, helping the coachee map and review the quality of key relationships and on building dialogue skills. The third coach focuses on the organisation, guiding the coachee to considering himself as an actor in the broader system. Over a period of two to three days the coaches and coachee engage in an intense process of dialogue, reflection, and discovery. This approach to coaching is based on a holistic and systemic view of the person. In the several months leading up to the process, the 'individual' coach guides the coachee in completing an extensive battery of instruments that generate insights on individual traits. At the same time the 'relationship' coach conducts interviews with people who routinely interact with the coachee, gathering qualitative input from multiple stakeholders. In parallel the 'organizational' coach gathers information about context, challenges facing the industry, the market, the company, the function, and this leader. What is the strategy? What are the goals and metrics? What is the culture here? Who is successful and why?

Over two to three days each coach meets individually with the coachee to present and review the information they collected. Then all three coaches meet simultaneously with the coachee to engage in a more integrated dialogue. The goal is not to *tell* the coachee what all the information means, but to facilitate the coachee's own meaning making, encouraging the coachee in a process of exploration and discovery. By the end of the intervention, the coachee is not held hostage to creating goals or development plans. Instead, he is asked to draft just a few simple sentences about was most meaningful, and what seems to be emerging in terms of purpose. The leader then returns to his busy world. Over the next nine to twelve months the coaches continue to hold periodic individual meetings with the coachee, joint meetings, and to facilitate meetings between the coachee and selected key relationships in the organisation. Through it all, the coaches collaborate frequently, shaping their approach and dialogue to best serve the needs of the coachee.

Summary

In this chapter, we have outlined various approaches the systemic coach might experiment with when asked to work with an individual. There are lots of other ways you might choose to engage with the system and we encourage you to get creative. What approaches you play with don't matter. What matters, if you seek to operate systemically, is the perspective you take with you into your work.

Notes

1 Lawrence, P. & Whyte, A. (2014). What is coaching supervision and is it important? *Coaching: An International Journal of Theory, Research and Practice*, 7(1), 39–55.
2 Kahn, M.S. (2014). *Coaching on the Axis*. Karnac: London.

Coaching Teams and Groups

This chapter is written especially for people starting out in the group/team coaching space. We hope it will help you make sense of an area of coaching that remains somewhat confusing. We hope it will help you get started, to find a perspective upon which to base your initial forays into this area. Reports suggest that team coaching is *30 years* behind individual coaching in terms of definitions, training and research.[1]

There are at least 130 different models of team performance out there.[2] Few of those models are evidence-based; of more than 500 research papers published on coaching in 2009, just six addressed 'team coaching'.[3][4] There are lots of people doing 'team coaching', but they're not all doing the same thing.

We suggest there are five generic approaches to coaching teams and groups, each building on the other to create an ever more sophisticated approach. Traditional coaches, upon being asked to work with teams, are likely to leverage their foundation *one-to-one coaching skills*. If they have *facilitation* experience they are likely to leverage these skills too, in building quite a structured approach to working with teams and groups. The dialogic coach, recognising that she is de facto part of the process, will be alert to the quality of *dialogue* in the room and will attend to creating a space in which new meaning is likely to emerge from the collective interaction. The systemic coach will have access to models that allow her to understand *team and group dynamics*, and will seek to understand how those dynamics influence and are influenced by events outside the team or group itself within the broader *system*.

What do experienced team and group coaches do?

The best place to begin looking for inspiration is often talking to those who go before us. We recently spoke to 40 coaches with an average of 13 years' experience working with teams and/or groups.[5] The coaches said they spent an average of 25 per cent of their time working with collectives. We asked them about their favourite theories and got them to tell us stories about their work. Between them they came up a long list of models and theories, and described quite different approaches to their practice.

Group coaching

The first question we sought to answer was, in practical terms, what's the difference between a team and a group? Having read the classic Katzenbach and Smith article, we thought we knew the answer.[6] Katzenbach and Smith make a clear distinction between teams and groups. Teams have a common purpose, while groups are made up of people with only individual goals; there is nothing that everyone needs to work on together. The mutual accountability of a team demands a set of disciplines through which people work together effectively, while groups don't. Sound familiar?

Not everyone subscribes to this distinction. Ninety per cent of the people we spoke to distinguished between teams and groups broadly on the same lines as Katzenbach and Smith, but 10 per cent didn't.[7] For example, one person said,

'I always try to get the group to decide on a collective task, otherwise there's no point.' For those people who did make a distinction, team and group coaching are quite different. For them team coaching is about working with an intact team, helping them to become more effective. Group coaching is undertaken with the specific purpose of learning. For example, one interviewee said, 'I see the group as a controlled laboratory for consolidating individual themes, a collaborative learning environment.'

We like this positioning of group coaching. In some organisations, we see group coaching being used instead of one-to-one coaching because it's cheaper. This is group coaching as a poor man's version of 'proper' coaching. When groups are run essentially as a series of one-to-one coaching conversations then this is how group coaching is likely to feel; participants may bemoan that they're not having their needs met, they're not being intellectually stimulated and they're receiving less individualised attention.[8] The traditional coach may go first to this format, using a combination of coaching and facilitation skills.

The dialogic coach, based on a belief that changes emerge from dialogue, and recognising the potential value of having so many internal perspectives in the room at the same time, is likely to run sessions differently. Dialogic coaches may or may not leverage facilitation skills to bring some structure to the session, but their primary focus is on creating a space in which people relate directly with each other. This is group coaching as a distinct form of intervention that has many advantages over individual coaching. We have worked on programmes where participants experience both individual and group coaching. People tend to appreciate individual coaching for the opportunity to share things that they simply wouldn't share with anyone else in the organisation. But people often get most out of group coaching, because of the value they derive from having time to relate with their colleagues in a dialogic space. Their colleagues have a diversity of perspective and experience gained from working in the same environment they do, a diversity of perspective and experience no individual coach can provide.

As we said at the beginning of this chapter, there hasn't been much research conducted in the team/group space, but early studies suggest that group coaching brings a dimension to individual learning that dyadic coaching doesn't.[9] Certain formats offer a level of intensity, focus and support not often found in individual coaching.[10] Early evidence suggests that group coaching can help participants become more confident, capable and skilled, more self-aware, better able to manage emotions and conflict, less physically and psychologically isolated, more appreciative of diversity and more aware of what is expected of them by their organisation.[11]

Group coaching is a place to get creative. The group coaching community has invented many different formats and structures. For us, the most important attribute of a good group coach isn't about great structure, it's about adopting a dialogic perspective. It doesn't matter what format you use, if you go into a group coaching scenario thinking that it's your job (as the professional coach) to do all the coaching, then not everyone is going to enjoy themselves. Some people will stay focused and energised, alert to what they can learn from your conversations with others in the group, but the majority will probably get bored. The dialogic coach, who truly believes that insights and change will emerge unpredictably from the interaction between members of the group, is more likely to run a successful session regardless of the structure used. That said, here are just a couple of structures we've seen used. There are many more to choose from; just do some reading and meet up with other group coaches if this an area of your practice you seek to develop.

Turn-taking

One of the questions we always ask our groups is – do you all want to be coached in every session? Remember, if this is group coaching as opposed to team coaching, then people are coming to the group with individual goals. If you're working with people from the same organisation this may change over the life of the group: people may discover they are all working on similar challenges, and the nature of the intervention may evolve more into a team coaching format. But to begin with you are likely to start with individual goals. So long as your sessions are collaborative and participative, your group may be happy to take turns from session to session. Whether that's achievable will depend on how many are in the group and how long you must coach, of course, but in such cases, you may choose a structured approach.

For example, we coached a group of six senior managers in a government organisation, just recently. Each session was scheduled to run for no more than three hours and the group was quite clear they wanted everyone to get a go at every session. They felt this was particularly important for at least the first few sessions; group members didn't know each other well and they were unsure how much to share with each other. No one felt comfortable being asked to disclose sensitive issues unless everyone was going to participate. In the first session, we talked about various formats we could use and the group came up with the following structure that everyone would experience, one by one. Bob went first.

0–5 minutes	Bob described his issue while everyone else listened.
5–10 minutes	Everyone else in the group asked one question of Bob, to which Bob replied.
10–20 minutes	Everyone in the group, except Bob, discussed the issue while Bob listened.
20–25 minutes	Each person in the group shared their thoughts with Bob while Bob listened, without responding.
25–30 minutes	Bob told the group what he had experienced while listening to them talk, shared what insights he had gained, and told the group what actions he was committing to.

A few things to discuss here! First, although the structure obliges group members to talk to each other, it isn't necessarily dialogic. In Chapter 2 we defined dialogue as one type of conversation, in which participants suspend judgement and voice courageously. A *traditional* coach with facilitation experience would likely use this structure differently than would the *dialogic* coach. For example, the dialogic coach could provide a short lesson on dialogue and invite the group to contract to adopting some dialogic principles. So, when everyone in the group takes turns to ask Bob questions, what kind of questions get asked? Do the questions imply open-minded curiosity? Or advice-in-disguise? An example of a question that appears to reflect open-minded curiosity might be 'What's the hardest aspect of this issue for you?' An example of 'advice-in-disguise' is 'I'm wondering – have you considered the possibility that none of your team know what the organisation wants from them, and that your best course of action would be to have an away-day at which you spell out the strategic objectives of the organisation, clearly linking those objectives to the role that they play in the team?'

The dialogic coach may pay attention to the extent to which the group is successfully co-creating the conditions for effective dialogue. In this example, the coach asked participants at the end of the session how they had experienced the conversation. Regarding 'dialogue', he asked people to what extent they felt they had succeeded in 'suspending' judgement vs. feeling compelled to offer advice. He asked them to what extent they felt they had co-created a space in which people felt safe to disclose and to challenge. Sue, another member of the group, nodded at Harry and thanked him for sharing the anxieties he was experiencing in managing his issue, and for trusting the group with his story. Having shared her issue first, she confessed to having held back and committed to being more courageous in future sessions.

The second talking point we'll highlight here is how the group coaching format might challenge the beliefs of a traditional coach. In this format, it is the other members of the group who are effectively 'coaching' Bob. It's unlikely they will demonstrate outstanding coaching skills and the traditional coach may feel an urge to step in and show them how to coach 'properly'. Also, Bob gets to talk for less than half the time. This may not sit well with the traditional coach who believes that it's the coachee who should be doing at least 80 per cent of the talking. And, towards the end, the rest of the group are specifically encouraged to give Bob advice. Is that really coaching?

These are some of the issues you will need to consider for yourself in deciding for yourself how you want to coach groups. It serves to highlight however that the dialogic approach is not the same as the traditional approach. In our view, the traditional approach absolutely supports the importance of 'good' listening. To us it seems more hesitant on the role of good voicing.

Coaching the coach

As we said before, the group coach gets creative in designing formats that will work best in particular situations. We worked for an organisation last year who wanted us to coach groups, while at the same time helping group members to become better coaches themselves. We were asked to work with groups of up to six people and told that each session would run for no more than 90 minutes. For us this precluded giving everyone the opportunity to be coached in every session, because we didn't believe we could achieve our objectives by offering each person just 10 to 15 minutes in the coachee seat.

We settled on a format whereby two or three people would receive coaching in each session. The first session was mostly teaching, the coach outlining basic coaching skills. In sessions two and three a standard format was used. In that format two members of the group coached a third member of the group while the remaining three members observed. The two coaches agreed between them how they would operate, eventually settling on a tag-team format. They found the tag-team format worked better than attempting to co-coach because it enabled each coach to stay 'in flow'. Half way through the session we called a time-out and asked the observers to provide the coaches with feedback on their coaching skills. The coaches had the opportunity to make sense of the feedback and to decide on what they would do differently in the second half of the conversation. The observers were again asked to give feedback at the end. Each coaching scenario went for 20 to 50 minutes depending on the energy in the room.

Again, this format might work well for a traditional coach with facilitation experience. The traditional coach would likely emphasise the teaching of coaching skills and holding people to account in implementing those skills effectively. The dialogic coach is likely to be less attached to ensuring people coach as they are 'supposed' to. The dialogic coach, being cognisant of contemporary change theory (as outlined in Chapter 3), is curious about what sense people make of what got taught. Every organisation, every culture, every group of people is different. What model of 'coaching' will work best for this group? Dialogic coaches are more likely to encourage the group to explicitly question and review its own model for coaching than they are to hold the group to account to the version of coaching presented. Heresy?

Something strange happened with this group. By the end of session five they declared themselves bored with the format they had chosen; it no longer served a purpose. Instead they reflected on how much they appreciated having created a safe, supportive space in which to tackle issues together. They talked about the organisation and how recent restructuring seemed to have driven people to focus solely on their own deliverables. Siloes had appeared, which were getting in the way of delivering on the organisation's biggest objectives. They decided to take it on themselves to lead the organisation back to a more collaborative way of working. They aligned around this common purpose and started coming up with some immediate areas of focus. In other words, the learning group transformed itself into a team . . .

What do experienced team and group coaches do? (part 2)

Let's now turn to team coaching. Of the 40 people we spoke to, 36 were experienced team coaches. Every one of those coaches said that coaching individuals is very different to working with teams because team coaches work with 'process'. This may sound familiar – the ability of the team coach to work with 'process' – but what does that word process mean? The coaches we spoke to used the word to mean different things.

Process as TASK

Process as task means focusing on the extent to which the team has clear objectives, clear individual roles, and clearly defined approaches to team meetings and decision making. Some team coaches believe that their primary role is to focus on task and to leave other forms of process alone.[12] They said they don't go near interpersonal relationships because this often gets messy and, even if it doesn't, rarely leads to improvements in team performance. They believe that by helping the team to define a clear purpose, clear roles and clear rules for working together, interpersonal relationships almost always improve as a result.

Process as TEAM DYNAMICS

Most coaches used the word 'process' to mean team or group dynamics. However, this only gets us so far. As Christine Thornton[13] writes:

> . . . people use the phrase 'group dynamics' as a kind of catch-all phrase when talking about several things at once, or a sense of 'what's happening underneath' in a group. Often the phrase is used when someone wants to convey that they don't understand what is going on, but have a sense that there is more going on than meets the eye. Because its use has become rather imprecise, the term itself has become less useful.

The coaches in our research spoke about team dynamics in at least three ways.

1 **Relationships**

   Just under 50 per cent of coaches said they focus on the way people interact with each other. This is clearly a different perspective to that of coaches who focus only on task.

2 **Dialogue**

   20 per cent of the coaches made explicit reference to dialogue. One coach said that his approach to team coaching consisted *only* of introducing a team to the principles of dialogue, then encouraging them to talk about whatever they wanted to talk about. David Clutterbuck,[14] Peter Hawkins[15] and Christine Thornton[16] all emphasise the role of dialogue in team coaching. An early David Clutterbuck definition of team coaching included explicit reference to dialogue: 'Helping the team improve performance, and the processes by which performance is achieved, through reflection and dialogue.'

3 **Developmental**

   Developmental coaches believe that teams go through developmental stages in the way that they operate, and tailor their approach accordingly. Several of the coaches we spoke to cited Bruce Tuckman's 1965 model:[17] *forming, storming, norming, performing* and, later, *adjourning*. One coach spoke with some disdain about Tuckman's model, suggesting there existed no evidence to support it. Some writers also question Tuckman's theories, notably Connie Gersick.[18] Gersick identified a pattern she called *punctuated equilibrium*. Punctuated equilibrium theory suggests that teams are only likely to be receptive at the beginning, middle and end of their time together.

Process as SYSTEMIC

All these approaches are in a sense systemic, and in a sense not. For while they focus attention on what's happening within the team they don't necessarily encourage people to think about what's happening outside the team. A team with a natural propensity to collaborate may behave quite differently if the organisational culture is hierarchical and directive. It may behave differently if key stakeholders are critical of the team's performance. Deborah Ancona and colleagues[19] suggest that most teams are too inwardly focused.

So, just as we suggested at the beginning of this chapter, group and team coaches all seem to be doing quite different things with their clients, based not just on different theories and models, but different approaches to coaching. This was all very interesting, not just to us but the coaches we were talking to. It was hard at times, to get the coaches to stick to answering our questions. Many of them asked us questions, curious to know what other coaches had said. Faced with this multitude of different philosophies and approach we wondered: can we capture these different findings in a model? Then we realised we didn't have to. One already exists.

The 'five disciplines' model

Peter Hawkins provides a framework for coaches interested in working systemically.[20] The model focuses on both internal and external aspects of the team's functioning (Figure 5.1). To be effective, he suggests, a team needs:

  (i) A clear *commission* from those who brought the team into being.
 (ii) To *clarify* its own mission, including purpose, goals, values and ways of working.
(iii) To constantly attend to how it works together in *co-creating*.
 (iv) To *connect* effectively with external stakeholders.
  (v) To continually stand back and reflect on itself (*core learning*).

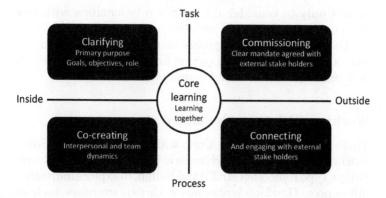

Figure 5.1

Reflecting on this model, we considered what the coaches told us, and we spoke to Peter Hawkins to better understand how he uses it. With most teams, he said, he starts with *commissioning*. Does the team understand what it exists for? What does the broader system rely upon the team for? To answer this question requires talking not only to stakeholders outside the team, but also stakeholders outside the organisation. If we're the IT function of a retailer, for example, what do our customers demand of us? If the team has a clear commission, then Hawkins suggests the team will most usefully consider what team members are committed to achieving together. What is it that team members must work on together if they are to satisfy their commission? What roles do members of the team need to play to achieve team objectives? Notice, this is a similar idea to 'process as task'. Whereas some coaches don't believe they have a role beyond 'process as task', Hawkins suggests we may then need to consider team dynamics. Indeed, if the team is incapable of having effective conversations for *commissioning* or *clarifying*, there may be occasions on which the work needs to start with *co-creating*. We can compare 'co-creating' to 'process as team dynamics'. The 'process as system' perspective encourages us not only to consider the team's relationships with key stakeholders (*connecting*) but also *commissioning*.

We find the 'five disciplines' model useful in talking to teams about possible focus areas for coaching, one of which is doing some work around team dynamics.

Working with team dynamics

There are many ways to work with team dynamics. Some coaches said they use psychometric tools, such as the Myers-Briggs Type Indicator (MBTI) and Belbin, to explore individual differences. Hawkins writes about various exercises such as the 'floating team sculpt' to explore the deeper dynamics of the team[21]. In this section, we'll briefly review two methodologies, both mentioned explicitly by coaches in our research. The purpose of this section is to provide a brief overview of each of these approaches, so you can explore further if interested.

Structural dynamics

The term 'structural dynamics' refers to a set of ideas developed by David Kantor[22]. The basic premise of structural dynamics is that the effectiveness of a team is a function of the quality of dialogue between team members. Structural dynamics describes a way of identifying and working with patterns of dialogue. Kantor identifies four levels of structural dynamics.

1 **Action modes**
    Everything we say can be categorised into one of four 'action modes' (Figure 5.2). When we *move* we propose a way forward, or invite someone else to suggest what to do next. When we *follow* we support someone else's move, not just nodding silently, but validating the idea and moving it forward to completion. When we *oppose* we challenge and correct the move. When we *bystand* we provide a perspective on the interaction, either with

Move   Follow   Oppose   Bystand

Figure 5.2

reference to other things that are going on, or with reference to the way that the team is operating. The task of the coach is to help the team notice its own patterns of interaction using this language.

When teams get stuck we can usually characterise that 'stuckness' with reference to the model. For example:

- When we see one member of the team moving and all the others following, all the time, we call this *courteous compliance*. Courteous compliance may look OK, but the team is unlikely to be very innovative, or responsive to scenarios outside the team leader's capability and experience. The challenge to the team is to liberate more 'oppose', to counteract 'group-think' and 'bystand', to enable an awareness of the stuck pattern itself.
- Sometimes we see *point-counterpoint*, a repetitive sequence of move-oppose-move-oppose. The team is stuck in monologue with team members focused only on advocating their own points of view, deaf to the views of others. The challenge here is to liberate the 'follow', a collective commitment to exploring other people's perspectives, and again the 'bystand', to draw attention to the nature of the stuckness.

- In the *hall of mirrors*, every 'move' is followed by a series of 'bystands'. Ideas are offered up but no one follows through. This team can break out of its stuckness by enabling more follow', a commitment to building on ideas and working through how those ideas might be successfully implemented.

Teams often get excited when we talk about stuckness. They usually recognise one or more of these patterns showing up in the way they operate. Introducing them to the action modes helps them understand how and why these patterns of stuckness are happening. The language offers them a non-judgemental perspective and the opportunity to break out of these patterns. There is nothing wrong, for example, in spending a lot of time in 'move'. If no one in the team 'moved', then there would be no action; nothing would happen. But if everyone is moving, all of the time, then still nothing gets done. There are lots of suggestions for moving things forward, but none are being challenged ('oppose'), none are being advanced ('follow'), and no one is providing perspective on what's going on in the room ('bystand'). The language of structural dynamics helps teams take ownership for their own patterns of interaction without resorting to blame-games.

2   **Operating systems**

We each have our preferred way of operating (Figure 5.3). Some of us prefer *open* systems with an emphasis on collaboration and participation. Others of us prefer a *closed* system, a highly structured way of doing things, with an emphasis on rules, processes and systems. Others of us prefer *random* systems, with an emphasis on creativity and individuality. Each system contributes to the functioning of the overall team, and each system, if over-played, can lead to the team becoming ineffective. Our preferences for different systems show up in the language that we use. The coach's task is to help the team notice how these sub-systems are showing up and how

Open   Closed   Random

Figure 5.3

they are contributing to the functioning of the team as a whole.

In teams where people have very different preferred operating systems these differences can show up as conflict. For example, George likes closed systems. This shows up in his desire to make sure there is a detailed agenda for every meeting. He likes rules and process because rules and process save time. He believes in the mantra 'if it ain't broke, don't fix it'. George gets really frustrated with Kelly. Kelly is forever undermining the agenda of meetings, always having to make sure everyone gets to speak, forever seeking consensus. Ellie isn't much better. Ellie drops little grenades into the conversation, thoughts and observations that have nothing to do with what's on the agenda. These tensions can become the basis for serious conflict, conflict that may derail the efforts of the team to perform. By helping the team look at this conflict through the lens of 'operating systems' the team coach again enables teams to talk about their differences in non-judgemental terms. All teams need some 'open', otherwise nothing gets agreed. They need some 'closed', otherwise they'll spend forever in meetings and constantly be reinventing the wheel. And they need some 'random', energy for thinking outside the box in search of solutions.

3   **Communication domains**
Some of us tend to talk in terms of relationships and the way people are feeling. This is the domain of *affect*. Others of us like to talk ideas, about why we are doing things – in service of what? This is the domain of *meaning*. And others emphasise results and getting things done. This is the *power* domain (Figure 5.4). Again, a focus on all three domains contributes to the functioning of the over-all team, and each system, if overplayed, can lead to the team becoming ineffective. The task of the coach is again to help the team notice how different members of the team express themselves and to develop a greater respect for people who express themselves differently.

Structural dynamics enables the coach to get curious about the functioning of the team in the context of the wider sys-tem. For example, I spoke recently to a puzzled team coach. She had profiled each individual team member and found that they all preferred *open* or *random* systems and they all had a strong propensity to either *follow* or *bystand*. Yet the team said that their overall team dynamic was to *move* in *closed power*. Only upon thinking more broadly about the organisational culture did this make sense. The senior

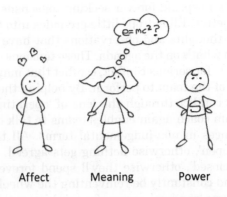

Affect   Meaning   Power

Figure 5.4

executive team were impatient for results and expressed little interest in talking about vision, strategy or how the organisation was feeling. They were directive and demonstrated little tolerance for pushback. This dynamic was manifesting itself in the behaviour of teams further down the organisation.

Bowen Theory

Just as David Kantor started out working as family therapist, so Murray Bowen's models were developed for working with family systems.[23] Bowen focused on patterns that develop within family systems to defuse anxiety. He developed techniques to help team members become aware of how emotional systems were working inside the family, and to help people disentangle themselves from those systems. His theory comprises eight concepts, some of which are more useful than others to the team coach. For example:

1   **Fusion and differentiation of self**
    Someone in a 'fused' relationship with other members of the team is above all concerned with achieving harmony within the system. That person is likely to respond quickly to the demands of others, their actions directed at removing any perceived tensions in that relationship. Someone who is more differentiated within the relationship is more capable of making individual choices, even if those choices may increase the level of tension in the relationship.

2   **Triangles**
    According to Bowen every dyadic relationship is unstable to some extent. Anxiety arising in the dyad is triangulated out onto a third person, such that the triangle is in effect the smallest stable relationship. So, the team coach may notice that whenever the CEO disagrees with the CFO, one or other soon admonishes the Marketing Director, even if the Marketing Director hasn't actually said anything. Adam's boss George knows all about this. These triangles are most likely to show up under stress.

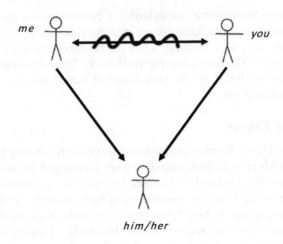

Figure 5.5

3 **Multigenerational transmission**

   In families, patterns, themes and roles are passed down from generation to generation through projection from parent to child. In organisations, a similar process occurs in which the leader of a team projects their approach onto team members, who may then unwittingly adopt that approach as their own. How this process works will be different for different people, but framing a dialogue around the concept may generate new insights for people.

4 **Sibling positions**

   Sibling position can provide useful information on understanding the roles different family members adopt. For example, the eldest child may be more likely to take on responsibility and leadership, the youngest child may be more comfortable letting others make decisions, and the middle child may be more flexible. The same patterns may emerge in organisational teams depending on seniority or length of time spent as a member of the team and/or organisation.

Bowen's ideas offer the coach useful insights. The coach may choose to share these insights with the team, if it feels safe to do so, and help the team to both make sense of their team dynamic and decide what to do about it. Or else the coach may take into account observed patterns when designing sessions.

Structural dynamics and Bowen theory are just two approaches that a team coach might use in working with teams. Whatever approach you choose, bear in mind Christine Thornton's advice: 'It is at our peril that we ignore the system within which our client team operates'.[24]

Learning how

In learning to become an effective group or team coach, of course we will need to learn new skills. Figure 5.6 suggests a learning pathway. David Clutterbuck[25] suggests there are two categories of team coach. The first simply transfer what they do in coaching individuals, 'add a dash of facilitation and or team building, and wing it'. The second start from a deep understanding of process and team dynamics, have a clear understanding of some of the ethical considerations in working with teams and distinguish carefully between team coaching and team facilitation. We look at things slightly differently.

We believe that *foundation* coaching skills coupled with *facilitation* skills provide the basis for getting started. The individual coach can also practice applying *dialogue* skills in a one-to-one relationship. Without these skills, the prospect of working with groups and teams may appear impossibly

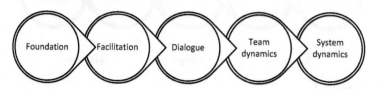

Figure 5.6

daunting. Yes, it would be great to have a working knowledge of team dynamics too, but these kinds of skills are hard to acquire without having a go. A coach with good foundation coaching skills and facilitation skills may feel competent to work with groups, leveraging structure to design effective learning sessions. Such a coach might even feel competent working with teams, so long as the team is clearly committed to focusing on task. As Clutterbuck suggests, to work confidently with teams with whatever comes up demands an understanding of *team dynamics*, and to be truly effective the coach will need to practice working with team dynamics in a range of different organisational *systems*. The extent to which the aspiring coach is likely to succeed isn't only about learning new skills, but also about choosing an approach to coaching (Figure 5.7).

As we discussed before, traditional coaches may find it challenging to work with groups and teams without questioning their approach to coaching. There are lots of coaching competencies you can refer to in working with individuals, and lots of places to go and get trained. There are far fewer resources and training offers available for those wanting to become effective team coaches. For now, you must decide for yourself what approach to take towards the work that you do. However, declaring our hand, we believe that if you see

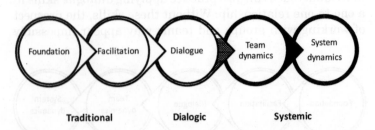

Figure 5.7

yourself as a traditional coach, you will find it hard to enjoy team coaching, or to be good at it, without first challenging your approach.

As we suggested, in challenging David Clutterbuck's perhaps dismissive perspective on individual coaching and facilitation skills, the best way to learn team dynamics is to work with teams. There are heaps of generic team coaching methodologies (more than 130, as we said up front) and lots of different approaches to working with team dynamics. It's hard to know which of these resonate best without trying them out, but how to take those first steps? Here, we absolutely recommend you find yourself a partner. Individual coaching is different, there will come a time when you need to take that first step into a paid assignment all by yourself. Not so with team coaching. It's common for team coaches to work together. Team dynamics are complex, volatile, dynamic. It's hard even for the most experienced team coach to stay simultaneously focused on the content of a discussion, team dynamics, and how what's happening in the room is a function of what's happening in the broader system. If you don't have a partner, or the clients you work with are unwilling to fund two coaches, then we suggest you get yourself a great supervisor, someone who has experience of coaching groups and teams, someone you trust to be your invisible partner.

Regardless of the development path you choose, let us share with you the final outcome from the research we conducted. Every coach said that one cannot rely on individual coaching skills alone when stepping into a room with a team. This is important. Sixty per cent of organisations think it's easy for coaches to transition from individual coaching to coaching teams.[26] Many team leaders inside organisations are attempting to coach their teams using techniques learned in the training they've received to coach individuals.[27] The coaching of teams and groups appears to be an area ripe for further dialogue, exploration and innovation. We suggest you find some partners to explore with.

Notes

1 Hawkins, P. (2014). *Leadership Team Coaching: Developing Collective Transformational Leadership*, 2nd edition. Kogan Page: Philadelphia

2 Peters, J. & Carr, C. (2013). Team effectiveness and team coaching literature review. *Coaching: An International Journal of Theory, Research and Practice*, 6(2), 116–136.

3 Grant, A.M., Cavanagh, M.J., Parker, H. M. & Passmore, J. (2010). The state of play in coaching today: A comprehensive review of the field. *International Review of Industrial and Organizational Psychology*. 10, 125–167.

4 Peters, J. & Carr, C. (2013). Team effectiveness and team coaching literature review. *Coaching: An International Journal of Theory, Research and Practice*, 6(2), 116–136.

5 Lawrence, P. & Whyte. A. (2017). What do experienced team coaches do? Current practice in Australia and New Zealand. *International Journal of Evidence Based Coaching and Mentoring*, 15(1), 94–113.

6 Katzenbach, J.R. & Smith, D.K. (1993). The discipline of teams. *Harvard Business Review*, 71, 111–146.

7 This difference in perspective is mirrored in the literature. Richard Hackman, for example, said, 'Although some authors, such as Katzenbach and Smith, take great care to distinguish between the terms teams and group, I do not. I use the terms interchangeably and make no distinction whatever between them.' [Hackman J.R. (2002). *Leading Teams: Setting the Stage for Great Performances*. Harvard Business School Press: Boston, MA].

8 Muhlberger. M.D. & Traut-Mattausch, E. (2015). Leading to effectiveness: Comparing dyadic coaching and group coaching. *The Journal of Applied Behavioral Science*, 51(2), 198–230.

9 Thornton, C. (2010). *Group and Team Coaching: The Essential Guide*. Routledge: New York.

10 Lots of references from INSEAD, including [Kets de Vries, M.F.R. & Korotov, K. (2007). Creating transformational executive education programmes. *Academy of Management Learning and Education*, 6(3), 375–387], [Kets de Vries, M.F.R. (2015). Vision without action is a hallucination: Group coaching and strategy implementation. *Organizational Dynamics*, 44, 1–8] and [Ward, G., Van de Loo, E. & ten Have, S. (2014). Psychodynamic group executive coaching: A literature review. *International Journal of Evidence Based Coaching & Mentoring*, 12(1), 63–78].

11 Various references, including: [Aas, M. & Vavik, M. (2015). Group coaching: A new way of constructing leadership identity? *School Leadership & Management: Formerly School Organisation*,

35(3), 251–265], [Alrø, H. & Dahl, P.N. (2015). Dialogic group coaching – Inspiration from transformative mediation. *Journal of Workplace Learning*, 27(7), 1–11], [Cox, E. (2012). Managing emotions at work: How coaching affects retail support workers' performance and motivation. *International Journal of Evidence Based Coaching and Mentoring*, 10(2), 1–18], [Kutzhanova, N., Lyons, T.S. & Lichtenstein, G.A. (2009). Skill-based development of entrepreneurs and the role of personal and peer group coaching. *Enterprise Development Economic Development Quarterly*, 23(3), 193–210], [Scamardo, M. & Harnden, S.C. (2007). A manager coaching group model. *Journal of Workplace Behavioral Health*, 22(2–3), 127–143] and [Stelter, R., Nielsen, G. & Wikman, J.M. (2011). Narrative collaborative group coaching develops social capital – a randomised control trial and further implications of the social impact of the intervention. *Coaching: An International Journal of Theory, Research and Practice*, 4(2), 123–137].

12 For example, Edgar Schein wrote that practitioners should focus on team dynamics only with explicit agreement from team members [Schein, E.H. (1999). *Process Consultation Revisited*. Addison-Wesley: New York, Cambridge, MA]. Wageman et al. advise coaches not to address personal relationships at all. In their view performance drives the quality of relationships, not the other way around. Focusing on personal relationships, they say, may be engaging and enjoyable, but is unlikely to lead to improvements in performance [Wageman, R., Nunes, D., Burruss, J. & Hackman, J.R. (2008). *Senior Leadership Teams: What it Takes to Make them Great*. Harvard Business School: Boston, MA]. Slobodnik & Wile however, suggest that the *only* way to change a team's behaviour is to address the social system [Slobodnik, A. & Wile, K. (1999), Taking the teeth out of team traps. *The Systems Thinker*, 19(9), 1–5]. Kets de Vries says that the coach's main concern should be 'what is really going on in the intrapsychic and interpersonal world of the key players, below the surface of their day-to-day routines'. [Kets de Vries, M.F.R. (2005). Leadership group coaching in action: The Zen of creating high performance teams. *Academy of Management Executive*, 19(1), 61–76]. Elaine Russo recommends that Wageman's team coaching model be amended to include relationship factors [Cited in: Martin, E.R. (2006). Team effectiveness in academic medical libraries: A multiple case study. *Journal of the Medical Library Association*, 94, 271–278].

13 Thornton, C. (2010). *Group and Team Coaching: The Essential Guide*. Routledge: New York.

14 Clutterbuck, D. (2007). *Coaching the Team at Work*. Good News Press: London.

15 Hawkins, P. (2014). *Leadership Team Coaching: Developing Collective Transformational Leadership*, 2nd edition. Kogan Page: Philadelphia.

16 Thornton, C. (2010). *Group and Team Coaching: The Essential Guide*. Routledge: New York.

17 Tuckman, B.W. (1965). Developmental sequence in small groups. *Psychological Bulletin*, 63(6), 384–399.

18 [Gersick, C.J.G. (1988). Time and transition in work teams: Toward a new model of group development. *Academy of Management Journal*, 31(1), 9–41] and [Gersick, C.J.G. (1989). Marking time: Predictable transitions in task groups. *Academy of Management Journal*, 32(2), 274–309].

19 Ancona, D. & Bresman, H. (2013) *X-teams: How to Build Teams that Lead, Innovate, and Succeed*. Harvard Business Press: Boston, MA.

20 Hawkins, P. (2014). *Leadership Team Coaching: Developing Collective Transformational Leadership*, 2nd edition. Kogan Page: Philadelphia, PA.

21 Hawkins, P. & Presswell, D. (2014). Embodied approaches to team coaching. In: Hawkins, P. *Leadership Team Coaching in Practice: Developing High-performing Teams*. Kogan Page: London.

22 Kantor, D. (2012). *Reading the Room*. Jossey-Bass: San Francisco, CA.

23 Jenny Brown's paper provides a great, and easy to read synopsis of Bowen's work. [Brown, J. (1999). Bowen family systems theory and practice: Illustration and critique. *ANZJ Family Therapy*, 20(2), 94–103].

24 Thornton, C. (2010). *Group and Team Coaching: The Essential Guide*. Routledge: New York.

25 Clutterbuck, D. (2008). Coaching the team. In: Drake, D.B., Brennan, D. & Gortz, K. (Eds.) *The Philosophy and Practice of Coaching: Insights and Issues for a New Era*. Wiley: London.

26 Hicks, B. (2010). Team coaching: A literature review. Retrieved from www.employment-studies.co.uk/system/files/resources/files/mp88.pdf on 5 November 2015.

27 Milner, J. & McCarthy, G. (2014). Leaders as team coaches? Insights from an Australian study. Australian and New Zealand Academy of Management Annual Conference, 1–14.

6

Coaching the Organisation

As coaches with group skills, we get asked to teach internal staff to coach, often in service of creating a 'coaching culture'. We know a lot of other coaches and organisations who do the same kind of work, and over the years we have become aware that people adopt very different approaches. These differences can be articulated with reference to the three coaching approaches.

Traditional coaches likely view their task as being to teach coaching as a set of competencies. They know what coaching is and they work to that definition. They see their role as being to impart their expert knowledge and hope that participants will then go and implement their newfound skills at the end of the workshop.

Dialogic coaches focus on the group. They like to work with no more than about a dozen people at a time, knowing that dialogue is hard to facilitate with larger groups. They design their workshops to leverage the expertise and perspective of everyone in the group, recognising that there exist many different models of coaching. They recognise they may have less expertise than anyone else in the room as to the functioning of the organisation, and are curious to see what sense participants make of the materials presented. And they welcome the opportunity to help groups work through questions such as:

- What's wrong with throwing in a bit of advice?
- Won't people get annoyed if I start asking them lots of questions?
- Will my manager support this new behaviour?

Dialogic coaches understand that they may not have the best answer to questions like these in the context of a specific workplace, and will likely encourage dialogue among participants to help them work out how best to coach in their context.

Systemic coaches also focus on the group, but on the group as an element of the broader system. The systemic coach is less interested in whether participants demonstrate text-book coaching behaviours and more interested in whether the learning intervention is having the desired impact from an organisational perspective. In effect, the systemic coach is thinking about culture change. The systemic coach is likely asking:

- How is what's happening inside the room a reflection of what happens outside the room?
- If this intervention is to be successful, other than the people in this group, who else needs to engage in dialogue and who do they need to engage in dialogue with?
- What else will do we need to do to have the desired impact on the system?

Building a coaching culture is a change project

If your purpose is to help leaders inside an organisation coach better, then you are engaged in a change project; your role is to facilitate a widespread change in behaviour. If you think that's obvious – well we're not so sure. We have met plenty of trainers/facilitators in the leadership development space generally who appear to see their role as being to impart knowledge. The extent to which participants choose to listen, or to make changes based on lessons learned, is a matter for the participant, and for the organisation in terms of rewarding and supporting new behaviours and discouraging old behaviours. This 'knowledge transfer' approach to teaching coaching behaviours typically comprises didactic-type workshops and a recommendation that senior executives get coached themselves. By being coached themselves, senior executives will come to understand the value of coaching, and actively advocate the behaviour in others. Skills taught are likely to be generic. After all – a coach, is a coach, is a coach, is a coach.[1]

In Chapter 3 we provided a brief overview of contemporary change theory. You may recall us describing change as a social process, one in which people make their own meaning of what is being communicated to them. Change in a complex organisation cannot be controlled; we can only hope to influence and guide, and to influence and guide we need to participate in those dialogues from which change is most likely to emerge. This perspective again may help us understand why many efforts to instil 'coaching cultures' don't succeed. Many such programmes are based on a 'just coach' + 'train managers' = coaching culture' approach, and it doesn't work, even though you'll find it cited in books and articles. Here's an example[2] of such a model – there are plenty more:

1 Engage the client.
2 Show what coaching can do.
3 Spread coaching throughout the organisation.
4 Consolidate change.
5 Track, and celebrate success.

Organisations 'show what coaching can do' by providing everyone on the executive team with a coach, then 'spread coaching throughout the organisation' by training middle managers. It is assumed that change happens as a result, which can then be consolidated and celebrated, thus encouraging others to join the party. This is the Mr Spock approach to change – highly logical, insofar as it goes. But what if the senior executives being coached don't really enjoy the experience? Or what if they enjoy the experience but spend little time reflecting as to why they enjoyed it? Or what if they enjoy it, but are so in awe of their coach's ability they feel discouraged from giving it a go themselves? Or what if they do try coaching themselves, but don't do it very well? And what if we train lots of middle managers to coach, but they don't make time to coach their direct reports? Or they give it a go and it doesn't go well, so they don't try again? Or their line managers discourage them? Or fail to role model coaching behaviours?

If 'just coach' + 'train managers' isn't enough, what *do* we do? The key to implementing a coaching culture lies in recognising that organisations are complex, volatile and unpredictable. People's behaviour is influenced by a multitude of factors, some of which you can predict, some you can't. And the way that these different factors interact and manifest themselves is doubly unpredictable. Because life is so complex and unpredictable we must seek to understand the impact of our efforts on the system as we go and be prepared to adjust and adapt. Before we consider a case study, let's consider a few good principles:

1   Purpose is everything.
2   Coaching in organisations is different
3   Make space for dialogue
4   Evaluate, evaluate, evaluate

Purpose is everything

In organisations these days, people get asked to do lots of things. For some people life is about ticking off checklist after checklist. You might persuade me to attend a workshop (though I reserve the right to duck out and make phone calls) but it's highly unlikely I'm going to spend the time, energy and heartache required to fundamentally change the way I relate to others. It's not that I don't care. It's that I have so many other things going on. So, this coaching programme has to be important. It has to be purposeful. And I have to see with my own eyes that direction-setters in the organisation believe it is purposeful and important.

It's not enough for us to talk generically about the benefits of coaching. For many people, that's nice-to-do stuff, and we don't have time to spend on nice-to-do. I need to understand why coaching is important to this organisation. In other words, I need to understand in what sense this is strategic. This means that, at some point in the process, the senior leadership team must align around a purpose for any coaching culture programme. So long as these programmes remain the exclusive property of HR, thy are likely to fail. Here are three examples of organisations who successfully articulated a strategic rationale for coaching:

1   **Company A – developing people**
    Company A was struggling with poor employee engagement scores. According to the data, few managers spoke to direct reports about their development. Employees felt disengaged and ignored. With this disengagement came poor performance, high turnover, and a reliance on external recruitment to fill key roles. The leadership team declared that the purpose of coaching was to foster a collective commitment to developing others.

2   **Company B – collaboration**
    Company B was a software development firm, driven by the need to keep up with rapidly changing customer needs and a savagely competitive market place. They shifted their business model from packaging single-instance software, to producing online, multi-instance software-as-a-service. But in trying to achieve this shift, they struggled. People found it challenging to get things done within the existing hierarchy, and resisted working with people outside their functional lines. Company B designed a holistic intervention, including restructuring

and reorganising, and a coaching programme focused on collaboration.

3 **Company C – feedback**

Within 20 years, company C went from start-up to thriving multinational. It had a great culture, with people evidently willing to help each other, uninterested in criticism and back biting. However, having grown quickly, the company had coalesced into different operating units. Relationships between some of those units were tense, but people didn't feel able to discuss those tensions openly for fear of offending others. The 'nice' culture that had served them well thus far was getting in the way. Company C's definition of coaching focused on the importance of people being able to give and receive open and transparent feedback.

These different purposes were ultimately reflected in how each of these organisations *defined* coaching. Generic definitions are of limited value unless they explicitly reflect the organisation's strategic intent. We worked with an organisation recently who invited all 160 leaders to attend a workshop – 12 people at a time. The organisation chose not to define coaching at the beginning of the programme, but it did define a clear purpose. It didn't define coaching because it wanted the leaders themselves to think through the connection between strategy and coaching. People defined coaching at the beginning of each workshop. After each workshop was complete, participants went back out into the workplace and experimented with new behaviours. They met up again with their cohorts every month to reflect on what worked and what didn't work. About a year later we asked those who were interested to come together for a one-off event at which they were asked to come up with a single definition of coaching for their organisation. The definition they came up with reflected the needs of their organisation, and the beliefs, values and experiences of people in that organisation. In other words, they came up with a definition that was purposeful for the organisation.

Peter Hawkins wrote, 'It is foolish to create a coaching strategy without first ensuring there is the requisite strategic foundation upon which to build it.'[3] With a traditional approach, this might mean examining the espoused objectives of the organisation and looking for connections between those objectives and my dearly held definition of coaching. With a dialogic/systemic approach, it is more likely to mean helping the organisation to consider deeply what behaviours will be required to deliver the vision, and craft a coaching strategy accordingly.

Coaching in organisations is different

There has been very little research done as to what makes a leader a good coach.[4] Writers in this area agree that the main role of the managerial coach is to facilitate the development of the people who work for them, but they are less clear as to how this is best achieved. Is it coaching if I spend all my time scrutinising the performance of my people and telling them how to do the job better? Is that the same as coaching John Whitmore[5] style? 'Coaching is unlocking a person's potential to maximise their own performance. It is helping them to learn rather than teaching them'. Many organisations set off down the training pathway without stopping to consider what coaching means for leaders as opposed to external coaches. They may adopt a Whitmore-type definition and just assume everyone gets it. In fact, many employees associate coaching with what happens at the local park on a weekend (dads shouting at teams of kids to run harder, stay in position, and pass the ball), or else think of it as training. In one organisation, we spoke to an employee who said she wished her manager would spend *less* time coaching her. She was a new-hire, recruited to travel around the country training sales staff. Her manager, she said, coached her in the design of every slide in her training pack. She wished her manager would just back of and let her design her own packs without wanting to manage every little detail. Just stop coaching me!

Most coaching definitions have been written with professional coaches in mind. They aren't necessarily appropriate for leaders trying to coach. There seem to be a generally held belief, among some professional coaches at least, that coaching is coaching, is coaching, etc . . . and that the manager/leader can be expected only to demonstrate some of those behaviours. The leader-as-coach is thus a poor man's professional coach. This is an easy perspective to adopt, coming from a traditional approach, but it isn't very useful. In reviewing the literature around managerial coaching, and thinking about our own experience, we came up with four areas where the role of leader-as-coach may be *tougher* than the role of professional coach.

1   Managerial coaches may need superb **relationship building skills**. Most professional coaches get to meet their coachees before embarking on an assignment. Only if both coach and coachee declare themselves satisfied does the relationship progress. And if one or other get a bit fed up during the assignment, they can duck out. Compare this to the life of the leader. Many leaders don't get to choose their teams, nor can they always move people swiftly along if things don't work out.

2   Managerial coaches must be good at **giving feedback**. Some professional coaches don't give feedback at all. They just ask questions. They might be required to help the coachee process feedback from someone else, but they don't have to give feedback of their own. Some coaches do give feedback, recognising that some of what happens in the coaching room may happen outside the coaching room, but most managerial coaches are expected to give feedback. Avoiding feedback can lead to breakdown of trust.

3   Managerial coaches must be agile. The professional coach may spend half an hour doing reflective meditation to get in the mood for having a certain kind of conversation. The managerial coach may need to have six different types of conversation within the same longer

conversation. Managerial coaches must be great at **contracting**, checking in on an ongoing basis to see if everyone's happy with what's going on.

4   Many professional coaches steer clear of coaching teams and groups. It's hard working with teams; it requires some understanding of team dynamics to do it well. But most managers have direct reports, who expect to be led in a certain way. The effective leader must learn **team coaching** skills, like it or not.

The dialogic and systemic approaches may be more attentive to these aspects of managerial coaching. The traditional approach, with its attachment to generic definitions of coaching, less so. Different organisations have different needs. And single organisations have different needs in different parts of the organisation. Consider levels of seniority, for example. Most research conducted so far has looked at supervisors coaching front line staff. In some contexts at least, front line staff may most value clear direction and performance-related feedback. A senior executive, on the other hand, may appreciate less being told how to perform their role, and appreciate more being helped to think through issues for themselves. What constitutes effective coaching in one scenario may not be so well received in another.

Culture is another factor we shouldn't overlook. We have both worked in Japan, and are familiar with the idea of *sensei*. *Sensei* means 'person born before' and is used within organisations to honour the wisdom of older, more senior, staff. In effect, it means 'teacher'. The very notion of *sensei* may create expectations as to the kind of support one person may expect from another, even at the highest levels of the organisation. All cultures are different, defined not only by country and ethnicity, but by the behaviours of individual leaders in their areas of influence.

So, what are we to do when working with organisations? How to navigate this complexity? Refer back to principle number one – 'purpose is everything'.

Make space for dialogue

Change theory again. You don't achieve change by telling people what to do, you achieve change by creating the space for dialogue and paying attention to what emerges. Yes, it's important for senior leaders to agree on the purpose of coaching and the need for a coaching culture. But the senior leadership team cannot then just step back and wait for the delivery of that outcome. Others in the organisation will have a different perspective. Do senior leaders then communicate, communicate, communicate? Or do they listen? Do they role model dialogue? People have to make their own sense of the world, and so any programme designed to build a coaching culture must make lots of room for dialogue, and must seek to engage key people in that dialogue. If coaching skills programmes are one vehicle for achieving this change, then one purpose of those workshops must be to facilitate dialogue. Think about what that means in terms of participant numbers, room set-up, programme agendas and who else needs to come and join the dialogue. And when people leave the 'workshop' what then? The effective practitioner will structure a programme around opportunities to engage in dialogue.

Evaluate, evaluate, evaluate

Consider again the nature of change – volatile, uncertain, complex and ambiguous. Change is constant and the outcome of dialogue is unpredictable. This means that programmes cannot be designed, implemented and reviewed in linear fashion. Design and review are best regarded as ongoing activities. Review must be constant and ongoing, affording the organisations with opportunities to intervene in the broader system as and when required to ensure best outcomes. Here is a real-life example of an ongoing evaluation strategy in action.

Xurtek[6]

Jacqui, the OD Manager, invited us to deliver a series of coaching skills workshops in support of building a coaching culture. We asked her what was the purpose of the work and sought to understand better the broader system within which we would be operating. Jacqui invited us to meet with the CEO, Denis, who said he was investing in coaching because the company was growing fast, yet had no successors to the leadership team. The purpose of coaching was to develop potential successors. He was less sure why Jacqui wanted to invest in coaching skills programmes. He didn't have any great *objection* to the investment; he just wasn't sure why it was important. Denis and Jacqui chatted a while, with us in the room, while she explained how the coaching programme would help more generally in developing people faster. Denis nodded and agreed, although we didn't get the sense he was fully engaged. It was clear that Jacqui was the primary advocate for the programme, the purpose of which was to: **develop successors to the senior leadership team**.

We didn't consult with anyone else on the leadership team at that stage. Jacqui described a somewhat disjointed executive team, located across different countries, primarily focused on their own deliverables. They met virtually most months and spent little time discussing broader issues. Denis made most of the big decisions by himself. This meant that the purpose for the programme was not universally understood. At this point we put in place a process to ensure we could understand the impact of the nascent programme on the organisation as a whole. We selected 30 people from different levels of the organisation, different functions and locations and agreed with Jacqui that we would interview them each three times, at six-month intervals, over the course of 18 months. This was our evaluation strategy.

Notice we weren't overly concerned as to how participants experienced the programme, not at this stage. We were more concerned to make sure we had an ongoing process agreed whereby we could discern the impact of the work on the whole organisation. Some of the 30 people were members of the senior executive. A few were participants on the programme. Others were people reporting to participants on the programme. Others had no connection to the programme whatsoever. Xurtek was planning to put every leader in the organisation through this programme with the hope that leaders throughout the organisation would demonstrate a new commitment to developing their people. The only way we could monitor the success of the programme in achieving its purpose was to talk to people across the organisation over a period of time.

First interviews

We conducted the first round of interviews straightaway. We discovered that:

1   Everyone said the purpose of coaching was to help people develop, and that the organisation needed people to develop quickly if it was to achieve ambitious growth targets.
2   Most people associated coaching with telling and giving advice.
3   50 per cent of those interviewed said their line manager 'coached' them. This appeared to include any kind of developmental conversation or activity.

These insights helped us greatly in designing the first workshops. Denis was interested, and brought Kim the acting HR Director, into the conversation. They recognised a need to engage the senior executive team in further aligning around the purpose of the intervention. But for various reasons, that still didn't happen. Over the next six months more than 50 people across the organisation attended coaching skills workshops in groups of six to twelve. Anecdotal feedback on the skills workshops was positive. We did persuade some members of the senior executive to attend the opening and closing of coaching skills workshops, where they usually struggled to articulate their commitment to coaching. We had the opportunity to speak to these leaders informally and learned that some hoped the workshops would help people work more effectively across national and functional boundaries. The organisation was heavily siloed, they said. A second purpose for the programme emerged, which we wove into the ongoing design of the workshops: **encourage people to work more collaboratively with their peers**.

Six months later

Clouds had begun to form on the horizon. The market was changing, becoming more competitive. Sales growth was flattening and the leadership team were heads down looking for ways to rekindle growth. We conducted the second round of interviews and discovered:

1   Workshop participants now defined coaching as a process by which managers 'help others to help themselves'.
2   People being coached (and not attending skills workshops) continued to define coaching in terms of advice giving. This included members of the senior executive. We spoke to the coaches to find out why, and learned that coachees were coming to coaching expecting to be given tips and advice. If they didn't get tips and advice, they stopped showing up. We spotted a latent purpose for coaching, still lingering at the highest level of the organisation, which wasn't consistent with the work we had been doing: **instruct people on how to do their jobs**.
3   Direct reports to the senior executive reported themselves increasingly dissatisfied with the coaching they were getting from their line managers.

Soon after – more change. Jacqui resigned. Then Denis resigned. Kim, the acting HR Director, moved back to her previous role and was replaced by a consultant, Mark. Happily, both Mark and Gemma, the new CEO, were keen to hear what had been happening and to support the work moving forward. Gemma recounted her early conversations with the business owners, who expressed a concern that the organisation was too hierarchical. From where they were sitting it seemed that members of the senior executive were too busy doing stuff and not busy enough thinking about what needed to be done. They wanted to see more delegation and empowerment, and Gemma saw the coaching programme as an ideal vehicle through which to communicate this message. A new shade of purpose emerged: **empower others to work more autonomously**.

This emerging purpose evidently clashed with the lingering definition of coaching we had unearthed through the ongoing evaluation process. Mark became a key relationship for us over the next few months, as Gemma struggled to get on top of a series of issues that continued to drag on performance. We worked with Mark to again tweak the design of the programme, but also to work out who needed to talk to who to further align organisational strategy and programme implementation.

Another six months later

By this time all coaching skills workshops were complete. Many of the coaching assignments were also coming to an end, though some still progressed. We interviewed everyone again and found out that:

1   Most people now defined coaching in terms of empowerment and internal motivation and empowerment. There were some notable exceptions however; i) some members of the senior executive team, ii) staff in the US and Hong Kong.
2   Programme participants were seen by others as being more self-aware, more likely to listen and give feedback, and more likely to frame issues with reference to the 'big picture'.
3   Only 55 per cent of people reporting to the senior executive said they got coached, compared to 86 per cent of people further down the organisation.
4   People lamented Jacqui's departure and remarked that the impact of skills workshops appeared to be diminishing without her support. She had been proactive in engaging in dialogue with people around the organisation helping them think through how to best apply their coaching skills.

Mark scrutinised the results with great interest and asked us to share our reflections with his newly formed global HR team. What did they need to do, they asked, to move the work forward? Did they need to provide more training? Did they need to send out reminders to people to do more coaching? Rather than provide them with answers, we engaged them in a day of dialogue. Thinking more broadly about their hopes for the programme and the need to engage the whole system, rather than implement a series of 'refresher' training, they decided upon a 'dialogue plan'. They reviewed the organisational structure, identifying where coaching was already happening and where it wasn't. They talked about whom they needed to influence and how that might be best achieved. They left the day with a commitment to engage specific individuals and groups across the organisation in a dialogue around what needed to happen next. Gemma, the CEO, asked us to share the results of the work finally, with the whole of the senior executive team. At this point we left the project, handing over our work to Mark and to Gemma.

This is not classic before-and-after programme evaluation, where we ask ourselves – did we achieve what we set out to achieve? This is evaluation as-we-go, seeking to understand what is happening in the broader system as we progress, and intervening where it seems useful to do so.

Summary

These four principles reflect both dialogic and systemic approaches to coaching (Figure 6.1). This is not a linear process. We are not suggesting we necessarily implement these four principles one after the other. Once we get going then our evaluation process will inevitably lead us to consider and reconsider the purpose of a programme, the most appropriate definition of coaching for this organisation, and who else we need to engage in dialogue. We need programme sponsors, able to intervene in the system as a whole and not just the 'programme', with whom we can engage on a regular basis. This approach makes no assumptions as to the stability of the system. As the business environment changes, so will strategic intent. People will come and go. Management will change their mind. The traditional interventionist may complain that 'management never makes up their mind'. The truth is that management usually do make

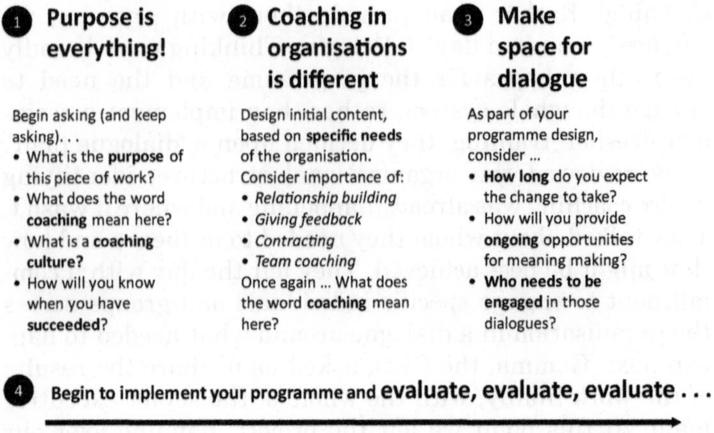

① Purpose is everything!	② Coaching in organisations is different	③ Make space for dialogue
Begin asking (and keep asking). . . • What is the **purpose** of this piece of work? • What does the word **coaching** mean here? • What is a **coaching culture**? • How will you know when you have **succeeded**?	Design initial content, based on **specific needs** of the organisation. Consider importance of: • *Relationship building* • *Giving feedback* • *Contracting* • *Team coaching* Once again ... What does the word **coaching** mean here?	As part of your programme design, consider ... • **How long** do you expect the change to take? • How will you provide **ongoing** opportunities for meaning making? • **Who needs to be engaged** in those dialogues?

④ Begin to implement your programme and **evaluate, evaluate, evaluate . . .**

Figure 6.1

up their mind – every day and in different ways – as things change and new insights and decisions emerge from the complex process of social meaning making. This is a messy and convoluted approach to facilitating change, as it has to be. Organisations operate in messy, convoluted environments, and so become messy and convoluted themselves. What is required of the practitioner is a willingness to work with ambiguity and what Clutterbuck and Megginson describe as an appetite for 'open-minded experimentation'.[7] 'There is no beginning. There is no end. There is only change'.[8]

Notes

1 Not our view, but this was the conclusion of [Hamlin, R.G., Ellinger, A.E. & Beattie, R.S. (2008). The emergent 'coaching industry': A wake-up call for HRD professionals. *Human Resource Development International*, 11, 287–305] after reviewing 37 definitions of coaching.

2 Bock, S. & Conlinn, C. (2011). When people really matter, organizations really excel: How building a coaching culture transformed employee engagement. *International Journal of Coaching in Organizations*, 8(2), 20–34.

3 Hawkins, P. (2012). *Creating a Coaching Culture*. Open University Press, McGraw-Hill. : Maidenhead UK; & New York US.

4 For a comprehensive review of the literature etc ... see [Lawrence, P. (2017). Managerial coaching – a literature review. *International Journal of Evidence Based Coaching and Mentoring*, 15(2), 43–69].

5 Sir John Whitmore is generally recognised as one of the prime movers in the executive coaching industry, and one of the initial proponents of the GROW model.

6 A longer account of this story can be found in [Lawrence, P. (2015). Building a coaching culture in a small Australian multinational organisation. *Coaching: An International Journal of Theory, Research and Practice*, 8(1), 53–60].

7 Clutterbuck, D. & Megginson, D. (2005). *Making Coaching Work. Creating a Coaching Culture*. CIPD: London.

8 Robert Monroe, according to Wikipedia.

Coach DEVELOPMENT

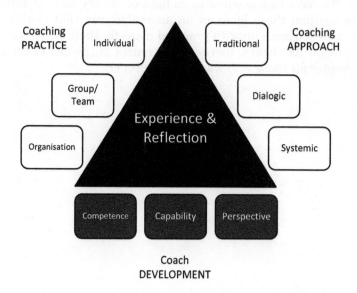

Coaching PRACTICE

Individual

Group/Team

Organisation

Coaching APPROACH

Traditional

Dialogic

Systemic

Experience & Reflection

Competence   Capability   Perspective

Coach DEVELOPMENT

Now that we've considered coaching *approach* and coaching *practice*, let's turn our attention to the third dimension of the model – coach *development*. Most of today's training programmes focus on **competence**. As we will see, to focus only on competence has its problems. We will also look at coach development in terms of **capability**. Capability is different to competence. Capability includes competence, but includes also knowledge, critical thinking capacity and learning agility. While competence can be directly observed and assessed, capability can't. The capable coach responds to the needs of the moment and makes decisions accordingly. Aspects of capability are invisible. Third, we consider the development of **perspective**, or the way we make meaning of the world. Building competence and capability are often referred to as horizontal development, while the development of new perspective, or sense-making, is to develop vertically. To develop vertically is to access new ways of looking at the world, to acquire new perspectives, to develop new relationships with complexity.

We have endeavoured to go light on theory and attempt to position these ideas in an accessible way that enables coaches to come up with practical plans for their own development. As always, there are references at the end of each chapter for those who want to dive deeper.

7

Competence

Coaching PRACTICE · Individual · Group/Team · Organisation

Traditional · Dialogic · Systemic · Coaching APPROACH

Experience & Reflection

Competence · Capability · Perspective

Coach DEVELOPMENT

Of the three aspects of coach development, competence is the most visible and obvious. Most coaching bodies have some sort of credentialing process, which entails one person assessing the skills of another person and declaring them to be competent (or not). This approach is common to other professional bodies too; doctors, architects and accountants, for example. This all makes absolute sense. If someone is going to remove my appendix, design me a house, or advise me where to invest my money, I want assurance that person has the right skills. So, does it make sense to adopt the same approach in the coaching world? Some say yes, others are not so sure. With reference to a wonderful article by the folks at Oxford Brookes University,[1] let's have a look at some of the limitations of a skills/competency approach to coaching.

1 Evidence
While there are lots of coaching competency frameworks out there, none are underpinned with a really strong evidence base linking competencies to outcomes. That's

not to say there's *no* evidence. The ICF's eleven core competencies, for example, were originally drawn up by senior faculty members from coach training schools, all people with lots of coaching experience.[2] These competencies have been (to an extent) validated by asking practising coaches to what extent they think these competencies are important. Those coaches asked, by and large, seem to like the list, though there may be some overlap between competencies here and there.[3] Asking coaches what skills they believe to be most important does constitute evidence of a kind, but who's to say the coaches are right? How do they know how their work is being experienced by others? There is little research as yet to support the idea that the demonstration of these skills leads to better outcomes.

2 **Complexity**

The focus on competence is traditional and individualistic. It's traditional in that it assumes that certain behaviours will consistently lead to particular outcomes. It's individualistic in that it doesn't allow for other factors that may come into play and 'mess things up'. A risk with this approach is that when things do mess up, and I am certain I have demonstrated all the right skills, I may be tempted to blame others. The coachee perhaps ('he just wasn't ready for coaching!'), or the environment in which the coaching took place ('that company just doesn't have a coaching culture!). Most coaching competency frameworks focus on the individual. Yet, as we saw in Chapters 2 and 3, changes in individual behaviour don't always lead to predictable changes in the 'system'. The individual is connected to a system of relationships. If we see change as a relational and collective phenomenon, then we somehow need to reflect that in our definition of effective coaching and in our models of coach development.

3 **Context**

The skills approach assumes the same skills will work best in every context. However, in Chapter 6 we reviewed

evidence suggesting that the skills required of a managerial coach may be different to those required of an external
coach, for example. Studying manager-as-coach, one
researcher found that of 12 coaching skills highlighted in
the coaching literature, only five seemed highly relevant
to the managerial coach,[4] while other evidence suggests
that the managerial coach requires more sophisticated
levels of skills in some areas than do external coaches.[5]
This is but one, albeit big and hairy, example of the need
to exercise different skills in different contexts.

4 **Over-engineering**
Many coaching bodies credential different levels of competence. But when I go to see my GP, I don't ask whether
I can see a level 3 qualified doctor, rather than a level 1
or level 2 qualified doctor. I might ask to see a more *experienced* doctor, or a *specialist* doctor, but that's different.
Yet many coaching bodies do gradate competence. This
means that i) they must reliably differentiate between
different levels of skill, and ii) they are assuming that
different levels of applied and measurable skills cor-
respond to different levels of effectiveness. Given the
challenges involved in establishing an evidence-based
set of competencies in the first place, this doesn't feel
like a *rigorous* approach. Rather it feels like unhelpful
over-engineering.

Conclusion

In our view, a skills-based approach to development is useful, to the extent that it helps everyone in the industry define
what basic, core, skills are required to effectively coach an
individual. For the newish coach, adopting a traditional
approach having a competency framework around which to
build a development plan is helpful. Attempting to define
multiple levels of competence within that single framework
doesn't seem so useful. In the meantime, many coaching bodies don't currently offer much to experienced coaches, who
want to become more effective working with complexity, or

who plan to extend their practice portfolio to working with groups, teams, and/or organisational culture. We need at least a couple of additional frameworks beyond competence, around which we can think about coach development.

Notes

1 Bachkirova, T. & Lawton Smith, C. (2015). From competencies to capabilities in the assessment and accreditation of coaches. *International Journal of Evidence Based Coaching and Mentoring*, 13(2), 123–140.
2 Barosa-Pereira, A. (2014). Building cultural competencies in coaching: Essay for the first steps. *Journal of Psychological Issues in Organizational Culture*, 5(2), 98–112.
3 For example [Auerbach, J.E. (2005). Inviting a dialogue about core coaching competencies. In Campone, F. & Bennett, L. (Eds.] *Proceedings of the Third International Coach Federation Coaching Research Symposium* (pp. 55–70). Lexington, KY: International Coach Federation] and [Griffiths, K. & Campbell, M. (2008). Regulating the regulators: Paving the way for international, evidence based coaching standards. *International Journal of Evidence Based Coaching and Mentoring*, 6(1), 19–31].
4 Anderson, V. (2013). A Trojan Horse? The implications of managerial coaching for leadership theory. *Human Resources Development International*, 16, 251–266.
5 Lawrence, P. (2017). Managerial coaching: A literature review. *International Journal of Evidence Based Coaching and Mentoring*, 15(2), 43–69.

8

Capability

Coaching PRACTICE — Individual — Traditional — Coaching APPROACH

Group/Team — Dialogic

Experience & Reflection

Organisation — Systemic

Competence — Capability — Perspective

Coach DEVELOPMENT

Experienced coaches know that multiple approaches to coaching exist. These coaches, in addition to mastering basic skills, i) seek to expand their repertoire of models and approaches, adding more 'strings to their bow', ii) make time to reflect on their practice, and iii) are committed to their own ongoing development.

These coaches may find themselves bumping up against competency frameworks, which seek to define single best approaches to coaching. So, we hear ongoing debates around goal setting, the extent to which the coach should explore the coachee's past, the role of advice giving, etc . . . However, continuing to debate what constitutes effective coaching solely in terms of skills may be somewhat futile. Many in the industry argue that there is a big difference between being able to exercise coaching skills, and being a good coach.[1] In these forums we hear people talking about coaching as a 'way of being', and the extent to which the coach's behaviour resonates with this identity. To what extent is being empathetic a skill, and to what extent is it an aspect of self? To what extent is being non-judgemental a skill, or a personal philosophy?

A capability framework encourages us to include a consideration of self in our development planning. If an effective coach is 'non-judgemental' then to what extent is it useful to learn a set of skills that may create the impression we are non-judgemental, when the little judgemental voices are still merrily chirping away in our heads? The coach is likely better off reflecting on her own 'system' – her values, experiences, beliefs, and identity, and thinking about how these aspects of self show up in her coaching. As we suggested in Chapter 2, our identities are not fixed, they are dynamic and they evolve. They are subject to every conversation and interaction we have. Once I welcome self-reflection into my development planning, then I become interested in ideas such as authenticity, self-differentiation and self-actualisation. As explorers of self we are embarked upon a journey with no end. Our potential is not demarcated by definitions of professional 'mastery'.

Measurement

Whilst we can measure skills and test for knowledge, it's less easy to decide how reflective and mentally flexible someone is. Measuring capability is harder than measuring competence, but there are people out there experimenting with new approaches. The team at Oxford Brookes, for example, are currently testing what they call a 'coach validation protocol'.[2] This methodology is based on the capability model in Figure 8.1.[3] This model defines capability as comprising four qualities. With some adaptation, we can list these qualities as:

1 Skills, or competence
2 Mental flexibility and self-reflection
3 Conceptual thinking
4 Commitment to self-development

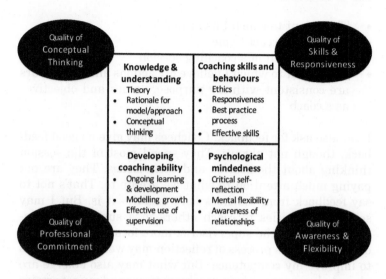

Figure 8.1

The process being tested includes coach observation, an interview and a written reflection. Assessors are looking not only at the coach's skills, but at their depth and breadth of coaching knowledge, commitment to development, and capacity for critical self-reflection. Time will tell what emerges from this work. We offer it here as an example of how some people are thinking, in practical terms, about how else to define the quality of coaching beyond competence.

Implications for coach development

In my efforts to become more *capable*, I choose not only to build competence, but also to acquire knowledge and to become more self-aware. How do I become more self-aware? This is where reflection comes in. Every time I coach, I have the opportunity to generate new insights into myself as coach. For example:

- The extent to which I feel capable
- How others react to me
- My enjoyment of a coaching session
- The extent to which I believe my actions and behaviours are consistent with my purpose, values and objectives as a coach

I can also ask for feedback. Coachees may give us good feedback, though not always. They spend most of the session thinking about themselves and their issues. They are not paying much attention to what we are up to. That's not to say feedback from coachees isn't useful – it is. But I may seek opportunities to coach others in a supervisory relationship, where the supervisor *is* more focused on what I'm doing. From this process of reflection may well emerge plans to improve my competence. But what may also emerge are plans to learn more about coaching, to expand my repertoire of mental models, and to consider more deeply how I can show up as the coach *I* want to be.

Notes

1 For example [Wang, Q. (2013). Structure and characteristics of effective coaching practice. *The Coaching Psychologist*, 9(1), 7–17].
2 [Lawton Smith, C. & Bachkirova, T. (2007). Manual for Validation of Coach Capability (version 6)] available on request from Carmelina or Tatiana at Oxford Brookes University.
3 Reproduced with permission from [Bachkirova, T. & Lawton Smith, C. (2015). From competencies to capabilities in the assessment and accreditation of coaches. *International Journal of Evidence Based Coaching and Mentoring*, 13(2), 123–140].

9

Perspective

Coaching PRACTICE

Individual

Group/Team

Organisation

Experience & Reflection

Traditional

Dialogic

Systemic

Coaching APPROACH

Competence

Capability

Perspective

Coach DEVELOPMENT

The third aspect of coach development is the least tangible and hardest to measure. In Chapter 8 we talked about capability. This is largely a 'horizontal' form of development, doing the best we can with what we have.[1] In this chapter, we consider instead 'vertical' development, or accessing different perspectives on the world, accessing entirely different *ways* of thinking.

In 1994 Robert Kegan wrote a book called *In Over Our Heads: The Mental Demands of Modern Life*. Kegan is a psychologist specialising in adult development. The basic premise of the book was four-fold:

1 Adult development is about progressing through different ways of thinking (or meaning-making, or perspective-taking).
2 To a degree, the pace at which we progress through those stages depends on the demands made upon us by the environment in which we operate.
3 The world is becoming more complex.
4 This places a demand upon many of us to progress more rapidly through those stages of development.

Kegan's account is primarily cognitive, and is not the only way of thinking about development. Ken Wilber[2] suggests that because *we* are multidimensional, so our development is multidimensional, and we develop at different rates across each dimension: cognitive, emotive, moral, spiritual etc . . . Each of these dimensions have a vertical aspect, in that they are not about how skilled we are, or what we know, but they are aspects of who we *are*, as people. This offers us a fascinating perspective on our development as coaches since it suggests that for us to feel more effective as coaches working in a complex world, we may need to *become* different.

Addressing each of Wilber's dimensions is beyond the scope of this book. We have chosen to focus on a cognitive dimension because various folks have suggested that there is a two-way relationship between the complexity of the work that we do and the perspective we take on the world. Even Wilber himself appears to privilege the cognitive dimension.[3] The cognitive dimension in this case, is not about intellect. Rather it is about our capacity to take different perspectives. This begs the question as to how we might access a different level of perspective-taking. First, let's look a *little* more at the theory.

Constructive-developmental theory

Constructive-developmental theories say that *development* in the way that we think and make meaning of the world is a *constructive* process. That is, the way we think isn't entirely pre-programmed or genetic (passive). We also develop in response to the demands of the environment in which we operate.[4] If the way we think is serving us well, then the way we think is less likely to change. But if the way we think stops serving us well, then we construct a new perspective on the world, a new way of making sense.

This isn't an overnight process, nor is it a conscious process. Vertical development is not a matter of motivation and effort.[5] Nor are there easy-to-use instruments that allow us to measure our own stage of development. In writing this chapter, we're very much aware that 'setting up an explicit task of moving the client through developmental levels of stages in a short-term coaching contract is, to say the least, irresponsible".[6] At the same time, however:

> It is the coach as a person, rather than the application of particular techniques or methods, that makes a difference in coaching practice. Therefore, coaches have to be aware of their own stages of development in order to reflect on their own role in the coaching process and the dynamics of the coaching relationship. With each new stage they reach, they become more capable of taking a number of perspectives on situations and of understanding more people.[7]

If we can't achieve new levels of perspective solely though motivation and effort, what *can* we do? The development theorists seem pretty much aligned around this one, the answer being to place ourselves in environments that challenge our current way of thinking. One of the basic propositions of constructive-developmental theory is that movement from one stage to another is driven by experiencing limitations in the way we currently think, and that this happens when we face increasing complexity in the world.[8] For example, when we come across a 'disorienting dilemma', a scenario we've never come across before, one that seems outside the limits of our current thinking. This concept sits at the heart of coaching in three dimensions (Figure 9.1), the idea that:

1   Our level of vertical development is an important factor in determining our approach to coaching.
2   Our approach to coaching is an important factor in determining the nature of our practice.
3   By pushing the boundaries on the nature of our practice we make it more likely that we will access different levels of vertical development.

But we get ahead of ourselves. What do we mean by vertical development?

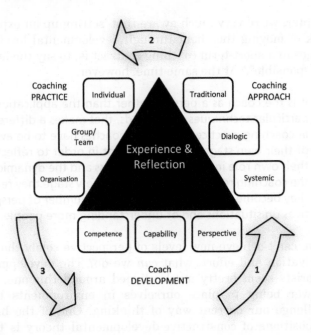

Figure 9.1

Stages of development

There are lots of different constructive-developmental theories and they use different labels for the stages we progress through,[9] but they mostly overlap to the extent that three broad successive stages of vertical development can be identified.[10] Here we'll call those three stages *reactive*, *independent* and *integrative*. We'll illustrate these with three quick sketches: Adrian, Bob and Carol.

1 Adrian (reactive)

Adrian works in finance, preparing month-end statements that tell the business how it's tracking. He's been working in this role for five years, working for a boss who gives him clear instructions as to what he needs to do and when. Adrian is conscious that the business isn't always happy with the information he provides. But they don't complain to him; they complain to his boss, Graeme. Graeme is the one who makes the final decision, and Adrian makes sure he delivers according to that mandate. Adrian and Graeme sit down every six months to review his performance, and his performance is always 'good' or 'very good', and so Adrian is happy. Just in the last few days though, Adrian's mood has worsened. Graeme is about to resign. Rumour has it that he, Adrian, is likely to be promoted. Which means that he, Adrian, will have to deal directly with the business and their complaints about the financial reporting system.

Adrian is anxious because his values and beliefs are not fully integrated. This means that when push comes to shove, Adrian will check in with 'significant others' to make sure he's doing the right thing. Graeme is currently the most 'significant other' in his work-life, and so long as he is happy, then so is Adrian. But what's going to happen now? Choices will have to be made, but how is he going to make those choices?

2   **Bob (independent)**

Bob is a peer of Adrian's. He doesn't get on with Graeme as well as Adrian does. Bob has strong views as to how the department should be run. If the company is going to be successful, then finance has to listen to what the business wants. That's not to say you always give people what they ask for. The sales team, for example. Some of their requests are ill-considered. The task with Sales is to sit down with the right people, work out what they need, and come back with a way forward. They may be happy, they may not, but Bob knows how to run a financial reporting function and he knows what a good reporting system looks like. Others don't. They're wrong. Bob was shocked when he heard that Adrian was likely to become his boss. Bob knows Adrian will do his utmost to keep the business happy. The problem is, you can't keep everyone happy. You have to do the right thing, not the most popular thing. If Adrian becomes boss, then the whole team will spend their every working hour chasing their tails. Appointing Adrian to the role makes no sense.

Bob has values, beliefs and opinions, the same as Adrian, but his are more fully internalised. Lots of people are impressed by Bob; he exudes certainty. Graeme unfortunately, isn't so fond of Bob. Bob doesn't do as he's told. He doesn't always listen well. The head of Sales doesn't think much of Bob either. She says he is a bit of a know-all. Asking him to think outside the box is hard.

3 **Carol (integrative)**

Carol is head of Sales. She has been in the role for 18 months. Sales were declining before she arrived and now the business is growing. Before she arrived, people in sales were at war with both the marketing team and the supply chain team. No one agreed on anything and so the client suffered. Sales made deals that proved impossible to fulfil then blamed others. Carol spent the first few weeks in the role getting to know people, understanding what their priorities were, and developing a sense of what would work and what wouldn't work in this market. She focused on getting people together and facilitating dialogue. From that dialogue emerged new intentions and plans that helped turn the business around. Finance are proving a hard nut to crack. Marketing have some great insights into how to segment the market going forward, but to be able to segment the market in any pragmatic way, Finance must be open to changing the way sales data is organised and reported. Carol knows that Adrian and Bob are both up for the Head of Reporting role. Adrian, she knows, would bend over backwards to give her what she needs, but she's not sure how well he'll be able to manage other stakeholders. She's worried he would find the job too stressful. Bob would be hard work. He has some fixed and old-fashioned ideas. She will work with either if she has to, but is gently probing Graeme to see if he might be up for looking to the market to bring someone in from outside, either someone who's worked in a leading-edge organisation in a similar industry, or someone who just thinks a bit differently from Adrian and Bob.

Like Bob, Carol can talk about her values, beliefs and opinions, but she holds them more lightly. She doesn't exude certainty, though you certainly get the sense she knows what she's doing. She is genuinely open to the idea that there are multiple ways of looking at the world. The world is a mysterious place, ever-changing, and so Carol too, finds her 'self' in a constant state of flux and evolution.

Onions and ladders

If you're already wondering – which am I? – Adrian, Bob or Carol, just hold on. First, we need to talk ladders and onions.

Ladders

Many theorists suggest we develop in linear fashion. Life, from this perspective is like climbing a ladder from one rung

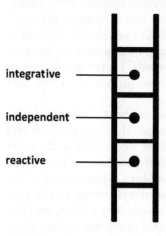

to the next. At each stage we access a new way of meaning-making, and step away from another, leaving it behind. They suggest that whilst we might *think* we experience ourselves on more than one rung at a time, one way dominates. Some theorists go so far as to suggest there are a series of micro-stages in between each main stage. So, if I am unable to decide between 'reactive' and 'independent' it probably means I'm sat somewhere between the two. There is no hard evidence

integrative

independent

reactive

Figure 9.2

however, to suggest that this is the way we develop, and coachees with whom we have shared these ideas find it hard to identify with just one stage. We know some researchers, too, have had problems in practice trying to categorise people in this way.

Onions

We prefer onions to ladders. The onion model feels more empowering. The onion model suggests that we *all* have a 'reactive' self that still shows up in certain contexts no matter what. So, in certain situations (e.g. presenting to a tough audience of 100

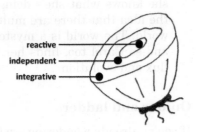

Figure 9.3

people) I find myself really, really wishing that everyone thinks I'm wonderful. In other contexts, I find myself thinking more independently, and even a bit more integratively. When I transition from 'reactive' to 'independent', my reactive self is not transformed into an independent self. Rather my independent self emerges and sits alongside my reactive self. In some contexts, my reactive self speaks loudest to me, in other contexts my independent talks loudest. In some contexts, they interact. In other words, I have an Adrian, or I have an Adrian and a Bob, or I have an Adrian, a Bob, and a Carol.

Authenticity, through this lens, is about getting to know these different selves, to what extent they are present and developed, when they tend to show up, and how they get along with each other. To have multiple selves, in this sense, is not a sign of mental illness. As Mary Watkins put it 'the hallmark of healthy psychological development is the progressive elaboration of different characters within, and the continuous enhancement of imaginal dialogues among those characters.'[11]

reactive me   independent me   integrative me

Figure 9.4

Jill's development as coach

If this is how adult development works, then our independent and integrative selves emerge in response to the demands made upon us by our environment. Let's go back and visit Jill and see how the story of her development as coach unfolds through this lens.

Jill, 20 years ago

Before becoming a coach, Jill worked in the corporate world, where she got most satisfaction from developing her people. She didn't enjoy so much the way that her company pushed for results no matter what, and she found the day to day pressure on performance unsettling. After a particularly unhappy few months, Jill took the plunge and started coaching for a living. She enrolled in her local university, which offered a degree in workplace coaching. The lecturers were fantastic; they knew so much and spoke with great certainty about how someone should and shouldn't coach. While studying, she built up her coaching hours so that she could become a member of a recognised industry body. She read up on their coaching competencies and made sure she understood their code of ethics, checking in with her tutors if something didn't make sense. Shortly after graduating Jill applied for and achieved the industry body's first level of credentialing.

Jill's reactive coach

Jill's reactive coach was pretty much alone 20 years ago. Her independent and integrative coaches were yet to emerge. Her reactive coach found client meetings challenging. It helped to have a good coaching CV. So long as the client bought into the importance of her qualifications and credentials, she felt fine. But some clients had strange ideas about coaching. For example, the client who told her that a good coach knew when to coach and when to stop and give advice. What he said wasn't consistent with what she'd learned in her studies. Nor did it resonate with the industry competencies she'd learned. On such occasions, she dealt with questions as best she could, before discussing the issue with her supervisor as soon as possible. When clients asked her to check in on how assignments were progressing, she made sure she spoke to the coachee first, to check with them what she could and couldn't say. Generally, she encouraged clients to speak directly to her coachees so she didn't have to get involved in the conversation.

Reactive Jill and her coachees

Jill met with prospective coachees before taking on an assignment, because that's what clients expected. Some clients invited coachees to meet with two or three coaches before deciding who to work with. Jill's reactive coach didn't like those meetings and found it hard to stay focused. If she didn't get picked, she got upset, and asked herself – what did I do wrong? What did the other coach do that was more effective? Once coaching started however, Jill was good at building rapport. She was keen to understand others' perspectives and quick to empathise, to the point of often becoming emotional herself. She followed her process, which included asking coachees for feedback. When a coachee said she was doing a good job, that was a great day. If the coachee was less enthusiastic, or hinted at ending a coaching assignment early, that was a terrible day. Jill restricted her practice to working with individuals. The idea of working with a group or a team was scary.

Reactive Jill and other stakeholders

Jill's reactive coach didn't like conducting three-way meetings with coachees and line managers, but did it anyway because she had learned how important they were when studying at university. She didn't like them because sometimes they didn't go well. Like when it was obvious that line manager and coach had different opinions on what the focus of coaching should be. After a three-way meeting, Jill always asked her coachees in private to decide what they wanted to work on. If the coachee didn't like what the line manager suggested, Jill always sided with the coachee, because that's how she'd been trained, and that's what made sense.

Summary

Not every characteristic of Jill's we've described is specific to her 'reactive' coaching self. A new-to-industry 'independent' coach may select one or two models around which to base their initial practice. Any coach may choose to gain qualifications and credentials in service of presenting a more credible front to prospective clients. An 'independent' coach may preference the needs of the individual over the needs of the organisation if that's consistent with their fully owned model as to how a coach should coach. What characterises this coaching self is a particular way of making meaning of the world. This coaching self of Jill's is very much driven by what others think of her.

- Do others think she coaching the right way?
- Would her teachers and industry custodians approve of the way she coached?
- Are clients happy with what she's delivering?
- Are her coachees enjoying their sessions?

It's not necessarily the case that absolutely everyone has to validate her approach, but significant others must. For example, if client and coachee are both agreed that the coachee's line manager is a weak performer, then Jill may be happy to proceed without that person's validation. If the client and line manager have forewarned Jill that the coachee isn't likely to respond to coaching, then Jill may be less concerned if the coachee doesn't engage with her.

Jill, ten years ago

Ten years on and Jill thought and behaved differently. She had had to navigate some tricky assignments over that period. Often the people from who she sought to contract disagreed with each other. Her coaching supervisor continually encouraged her to decide for herself who she wanted to be, as a coach. Her independent coach grew stronger. It knew how coaches ought to coach, and spoke confidently about best practice. Independent self likes GROW and CBC (Cognitive Behavioural Coaching), but has found other models and theories. Jill is still a member of the same coaching industry body. By and large she is aligned to their competencies and code of ethics. She sees these industry bodies as being very important – credentialing is a way of keeping unqualified coaches out of the market. She occasionally drops in at university alumni events where she mixes with other coaches and listens to her old lecturers present their latest insights. A couple of those lecturers she still thinks are great, a couple of the others she doesn't find so insightful.

Jill's independent coach and her clients

Jill now enjoyed client meetings. Occasionally she found herself caught off-guard when directly challenged by someone referring to a book or article she hadn't read. On such occasions, her 'reactive coach' felt threatened, and 'independent coach' had to deliberately intervene. This didn't happen often. The meetings provided independent Jill with an opportunity to talk about what coaching is, and what it isn't. She was happy to give advice on how to structure coaching assignments; how to evaluate the effectiveness of coaching; how to establish coaching panels, and so on. Unfortunately, some clients didn't know what they were talking about. For example, the client who told her that a good coach knew when to coach and when to stop and give advice. 'Reactive coach' was momentarily triggered, but 'independent coach' recognised straightaway that the client clearly didn't understand the difference between coaching and mentoring. Jill explained what each did and didn't do. The client chose not to use her in his organisation, which Jill's 'independent coach' decided was a good thing ('reactive coach' wasn't so sure). When clients expressed concerns about an assignment, wanting to know more about what is happening, Jill checked in with the client as to what she could and couldn't discuss with the coachee; then had the conversation with the coachee and relayed back the response. This approach, she explains to clients, was ethical.

Independent Jill and her coachees

Jill still met with prospective coachees before taking on an assignment, because it made sense. In independent Jill's view this 'chemistry check' process wasn't so much coaching as selling. She developed a message that she delivered to all prospective coachees, describing what is coaching, what to expect from a coach, and what outcomes to expect from coaching. She had lots of stories she could tel: success stories in which her coachees achieved great things by committing to the process. In the coaching room Jill was empathetic and knew how to put people at their ease. She focused on managing the coaching process, giving the coachee plenty of space to play. Some coachees really appreciated the structure she provided. Other coachees were less keen. Jill was constantly on the lookout for coachees who may not yet be quite ready for coaching, and she encouraged them to think about other development interventions. She generally got good results; her coachees and clients were almost always happy with the outcomes.

Independent Jill and other stakeholders

Jill felt confident working with other members of the coachee's organisation. There were things her coachee could be doing better and there were things the organisation should be doing better to support leaders in the organisation. She didn't find it hard to come to a view as to what needed to change and who should be doing what to effect that change. On occasion, she came up against line managers who didn't seem inclined to listen to her or the coachee. In such cases, she had a quiet word with the client and, when asked, gave the client advice as to how they might manage the line manager.

Summary

Again, not every characteristic of Jill's we've described is specific to an 'independent' coaching self. A 'reactive coach' may show up as confident and calm, even if challenged, if they have confidence in their teachers and coaching colleagues. The 'integrative coach' will also pick and choose the work they're interested in, though their decision is likely be based on a more systemic view of the coachee, the organisation and organisation's environment. What characterises Jill's 'independent coach' is the emergence of a particular way of making meaning of the world.

- She has defined a 'right' and 'wrong' way of coaching for herself.
- Whether clients are happy will mostly depend on whether their expectations are reasonable.
- Whether coachees are happy will depend on the extent to which their expectations are reasonable, and their commitment to the process.

There is nothing particularly significant about the ten-year gap it takes for Jill's 'independent coach' to emerge. Sometimes the 'independent coach' may develop slowly (or not at all) in that time frame, others may develop faster.

Jill now

Another ten years on and Jill is different again. With the help of a series of coaching supervisors she has come to see that her own model of coaching is not the only model of coaching. She had a couple of particularly hairy experiences coaching groups and teams, during which this became evident. She still talks a lot about her coaching model and is keen to share it with others, but she also enjoys hearing about how other coaches go about their work and is attentive to aspects of their practice she may integrate into her own. She is still a member of the same coaching industry body, though she is ambivalent as to whether clients should expect coaches to adhere to their norms. She enjoys meeting with other credentialed coaches to hear what they're up to, but feels a need to mix with other groups too so that her perspective doesn't become overly narrow. She enjoys hearing what others have to say and enjoys challenging others. Sometimes 'independent coach' shows her face and challenges others a little too forcefully! Jill's coaching feels quite intuitive these days. She doesn't consciously refer to specific models and theories, but knows that all of what she sources comes from somewhere! She enjoys supervision, formal and informal. She most appreciates the opportunity to engage in reflective practice, and regards supervision as a kind of focal point that helps her realise how her practice continues to evolve. Some days she feels really experienced, other days it feels like she's just starting out again. Jill's integrative coach is in charge (usually).

Jill's integrative coach and her clients
Integrative Jill goes into client meetings curious. She listens not only to the content of a client's narrative, but to the source of that narrative. For example, she talks to Mary, an OD manager looking for someone to coach a senior manager in her organisation. She hears a strong focus on accountability and integrity; doing what you'll say you'll do and sticking up your hand if you get it wrong. Jill gets the sense that though the assignment has been commissioned by a line manager within the organisation, she's really hearing Mary's own perspective on what needs to happen. Mary talks about the two previous organisations she worked for, organisations Jill knows well. Both organisations have a strong reputation for expecting their managers to deliver results. Jill's 'reactive coach' remembers an early experience coaching in one of those organisations, an assignment that didn't go well. Jill shivers and regathers herself. Jill understands that Mary

expects her to share this focus on holding people to account. Her 'independent coach' protests that this isn't coaching! But Jill probes further to see what other beliefs Mary holds. Though Jill doesn't share all those beliefs, she sees no problems working within Mary's high-level parameters. She asks Mary about the specific coaching assignment. The way Mary tells the story Jill thinks she can see where Mary and the coachee may be clashing. She tells Mary she is fine with the process in principle, but she'd like to check in with the coachee before committing.

Integrative Jill and her coachees

Jill's 'integrative coach' goes into sessions curious, listening not only to the content of the narrative, but to the source of that narrative. What values is she picking up on? What beliefs and life experiences? For example, she talks to George. Mary has asked her to help George become more disciplined and rigorous. As Jill gets to know George she begins to see the world through his eyes; through his way of making meaning of the world. George talks about the challenges he faces in getting people to do the things he needs them to do. Jill becomes aware of the respect he has for others, the way in which he will always make time to help others, and his desire to deliver what he says he will deliver. Others don't seem to share those values, which makes it hard for him to perform as he would like. He's feeling stressed and is thinking of leaving the organisation. He cannot understand why others don't conform to the same values he does. Jill's coachees appreciate the way that she listens without judgement. They feel validated and accepted by her. She is forever connecting dots, shedding new light on relationships, throwing up new interpretations to think about. Sometimes it feels a little uncomfortable to be coached by Jill. She sees things that her coachees thought were hidden. Occasionally a coachee might say, semi-jokingly, it feels like being on the psychiatrist's couch. But they always leave a session with a new perspective on themselves in the organisation and with something new to act upon.

Integrative Jill and other stakeholders

Jill's 'integrative coach' seizes every opportunity to engage with line managers and other members of the coachee's organisation. These interactions help her understand so much better the issues the organisation is facing and the way that the organisation is attempting to work most effectively with itself. These insights enable her to tune in more effectively to the needs of her coachees and the teams that she works with. When working with individuals she enjoys being in the company of coachee and line manager, noticing their relationship and providing feedback on her experience of that relationship when appropriate. She believes in the power of feedback, not as some sort of corrective mechanism, but as a means by which to enrich the dialogue through which the organisation makes meaning of its environment and its efforts to be successful in that environment.

Summary

Jill's 'integrative coach' is the most likely to adopt a systemic perspective. Once you start to look at people almost as different aspects of the same whole, and find yourself noticing that outcomes emerge from patterns of interactions; you can't unsee it or become unaware of it. Individualistic perspectives on leadership and outcomes no longer resonate. Jill's 'integrative' coaching self believes that:

- There is no wrong or right way of coaching. She is familiar with various models and theories, all of which bring value.
- Coaching is more a way of 'being'. It's about being curious, seeking to understand, and being able to share her observations and insights in a wholly respectful way.
- She will always have an impact on the functioning of the system. That impact is unpredictable. She can help others make sense of what happens, but she can't control that meaning-making process. Perhaps they will be happy, perhaps they won't.

According to this model, the more experienced Jill becomes, the more likely she is to find other aspects of her coaching self emerge. To begin with, Jill's 'reactive coach' is operating pretty much alone. Her independent' and 'integrative' coaching selves emerge later. These different selves can be compared (Table 9.1).

Jill is likely to become more confident and capable as she accesses new ways of perspective-taking, as her independent and integrative coaching selves emerge and develop. This is not a passive process because experience by itself is no guarantee of development. Jill can create a good environment for her own development in two ways. She can:

1   Commit to undertaking new and unfamiliar assignments, more complex assignments that are likely to stretch her 'reactive' and/or 'independent' coaching selves.
2   Make time to reflect on those experiences.

But that may be putting it too simply. Let's expand a little in our final chapter.

Table 9.1

	Reactive	Independent	Integrative
Primary motivation	Pleasing others	Coaching the 'right' way	Delivering great outcomes for the system
Approach to models and theories	Looks to 'significant others' for guidance as to which are most useful	Attached to those models and theories that best appeal to sense of self as coach	Engages, explores and integrates, as an ongoing process
Approach to other stakeholders	Hold at arm's length	Engage on own terms	Engage systemically
Personal practice model	Nascent	Developed	Evolving

Notes

1 Bachkirova, T. & Lawton Smith, C. (2015). From competencies to capabilities in the assessment and accreditation of coaches. *International Journal of Evidence Based Coaching and Mentoring*, 13(2), 123–140.

2 For example [Wilber, K. (2000). *Integral Psychology*. Shambhala: Boston; London].

3 Bachkirova, T. (2011). *Developmental Coaching. Working with the Self*. McGraw Hill: New York.

4 Cynthia McCauley and colleagues listed seven basic propositions of constructive-developmental theory:

   i People actively construct the way they make meaning in the world.
   ii People progress through different stages of meaning-making and these stages are common to everyone.
   iii Later ways of making meaning are more complex than earlier stages.
   iv People are often aware of the way they make meaning, but unaware of how people operating at more complex stages are making meaning. We cannot therefore reflect on these more complex stages.
   v People generally progress from one way of meaning-making to another in response to their environment becoming more complex.
   vi People progress through these stages in the same invariant order.
   vii People don't generally regress to previous ways of meaning-making.

   See [McCauley, C.D., Drath, W.H., Palus, C.J., O'Connor, P.M.G. & Baker, B.A. (2006). The use of constructive-developmental theory to advance the understanding of leadership. *The Leadership Quarterly*, 17, 634–653].

5 Bachkirova, T. (2011). *Developmental Coaching. Working with the Self*. McGraw Hill: New York.

6 Bachkirova, T. (2011). *Developmental Coaching. Working with the Self*. McGraw Hill: New York (p. 124).

7 Bachkirova, T. (2011). *Developmental Coaching. Working with the Self*. McGraw Hill: New York (p. 54).

8 McCauley, C.D., Drath, W.H., Palus, C.J., O'Connor, P.M.G. & Baker, B.A. (2006). The use of constructive-developmental theory to advance the understanding of leadership. *The Leadership Quarterly*, 17, 634–653.

152 PERSPECTIVE

9   For example, Robert Kegan, Lawrence Kohlberg, Jane Loevinger, Bill Torbert and Suzanne Cook-Greuter. For a comprehensive review see [Lawrence, P. (2016). Coaching and adult development. In: Bachkirova, T., Spence, G. & Drake, D.B. (Eds.) *The SAGE Handbook of Coaching*. SAGE: Los Angeles, CA].

10 McCauley, C.D., Drath, W.H., Palus, C.J., O'Connor, P.M.G. & Baker, B.A. (2006). The use of constructive-developmental theory to advance the understanding of leadership. *The Leadership Quarterly*, 17, 634–653.

11 McAdams, D.P. (1997). *The Stories We Live By. Personal Myths and the Making of Self*. Guilford: New York; London (p. 131).

Experience and Reflection

We've covered a lot of ground in this book, and challenged some perspectives. We've pushed hardest against the idea that the traditional approach to coaching, with its focus on the **individual**, is the only way to coach. It's a perfectly valid approach, but in a complex world, we argue, we need some coaches at least, to venture into the less certain worlds of **group and team** coaching, and we need some coaches to leverage their expertise to help **organizations** as a whole become more effective.

To become more agile and adept, coaches may need to consider different approaches to their work. The **traditional** approach, with its emphasis on competence, may not always suffice. The coach may usefully explore the **dialogic** approach in service of ultimately being able to work **systemically**. Working systemically means noticing patterns of relationships, and the emergence of new meanings from those relationships, even relationships that to us as coaches, may be invisible.

In the third part of the book we talked about three aspects of coach development. A focus on **competence**, or honing skills, fits well the traditional approach. To focus on **capability** is to focus also on expanding our knowledge set, extending our flexibility, and becoming more reflective. To focus on **perspective** (vertical development) is to reflect on how we think and to access new ways of making meaning. Adult development theorists believe that the way we think is, to some extent, an outcome of the complexity we face, and that for us to become more adept at working with complexity, the way we think and make meaning of the world must adapt and evolve.

At the heart of our model we have 'Experience and Reflection'. This the playing field upon which development happens. Experience by itself is of limited value without reflection. How often do we see people trying the same old solutions again and again, without success? How often do we find ourselves banging our head against a brick wall, hoping perseverance will lead to breakthrough? Whatever our developmental pathway, we believe that we learn most about ourselves through doing, and reflecting on that doing, but the focus of our reflection is likely to be different at different stages of our development (Table B.1).

Table B.1

Focus on	Theme	Focus of reflection
Competence	Skills and competence	Outcome of applying different skills
Capability	Skills/competence Knowledge Self	Above, plus desire for new knowledge, and understanding the impact of our own values, beliefs, assumptions and behaviours on others
Perspective	Self in system	Above, plus reflection on self in terms of the way we think and make sense of the world

Supervision

As we wrote this book, we shared drafts with lots of people. The question we got asked, time and again, was how do I go about developing myself? People weren't asking us how to develop their competence. There are lots of coaching skills training courses around. They were more curious about the idea of vertical development. We have said already that whilst motivation and effort won't necessarily lead to vertical development, and whilst vertical development is not an intellectual exercise, we may be able to facilitate our own development by engaging in more complex work. Some of you may already be quaking in your boots at this prospect. Are these guys really suggesting we take on any old work we don't feel confident of managing and just give it a go?

Our answer? No. We've tried that.[1] Not to be recommended. But we are saying that to become more confident working with complexity will require you to take a few steps outside your comfort zone. We would not recommend venturing outside alone. We recommend contracting the services of a 'coaching supervisor'. First, we had better define what we mean by a 'coaching supervisor'.

The history of coaching supervision begins with the importation of models from the worlds of counselling and psychotherapy.[2] Along with the models came suggestions that all supervision should be mandatory, an assertion that still generates tension in the coaching community.[3] The very word supervision puts off many coaches. It can evoke images of having someone standing over your shoulder, telling you what you're doing right and what you're doing wrong. Even now there exist multiple perspectives on supervision, such that many folks in the industry are just confused, with coaches being told they should go through regular, formal supervision without understanding why.[4]

As usual, definitions come into play. When some writers express concerns that most coaches don't get supervised, they are defining supervision in terms of formal practice, regular sessions with someone trained to be a supervisor.[5]

If we define supervision more broadly, as simply 'reflective practice', then our own research suggests that lots of coaches undertake supervision, albeit informally.[6] Whether you prefer a formal or informal approach to supervision, we believe there is value in making deliberate choices as to the purpose of supervision, and who you approach for supervision.

Different writers advocate different purposes for supervision. In this chapter, we'll refer to three possible functions, variously called resourcing, development, qualitative,[7] or formative, normative, restorative.[8] We'll call them **evaluation**, **support** and **reflective practice**. All three of these functions are useful and valid.

> *Evaluation* includes assessment. One potential role of the supervisor is to identify blind spots in the coach's practice, to call out skills gaps and ethical issues.

> *Support* is emotional support. Some coaching sessions can be emotionally draining and a potential role of a supervisor is to help the coach process those feelings.

> *Reflective practice* is purely developmental. The role of the supervisor is to facilitate the personal and professional development of the coach.

If we map the various needs of a coach against the possible functions of supervision we can see how important it is to be purposeful in seeking supervision, and the importance of contracting (Figure B.1).

Examples

Paul is new to coaching. He has worked a long time in organisational development, understands what coaching is, and has coached lots of people informally. He is about to step out into the world of professional coaching and start his own business. Though he has coached before, he's not sure he's been doing it right. He wants to work with individuals,

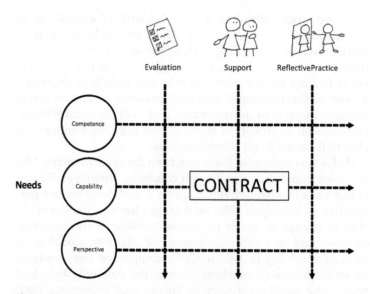

Figure B.1

and wants a credential as part of persuading clients he is a credible coach. Just starting out, he wants an experienced coach as supervisor, to help him understand and develop his coaching skills. He's looking for someone who is already credentialed. Paul knows he's going to find the transition challenging, and recognises the risk of taking on too many clients and becoming exhausted. He looks for a supervisor who can tell him if he's demonstrating the right skills or not, and who will help him through some of the more draining assignments. His focus on *competence* is steering him towards a supervisor who will *evaluate* his practice and provide *support*.

Mark has been coaching for several years. He's now venturing out into team coaching, an extension of his practice about which he is excited and a little anxious. He is looking for a supervisor who is already experienced in the team coaching space, who has a wide breadth of knowledge in working with group dynamics. Mark knows he is likely to feel challenged by working with teams, and already has some theories as to how he may be triggered in a team setting. He is looking for a supervisor who can help him develop a deeper understanding of self, and guidance on how to better manage himself in an uncertain and volatile environment. His focus on *capability* is steering him towards a supervisor able to function in all three domains.

Julie has been also been coaching for several years. She has done some group and team coaching, though still most of her work is with individuals. She would describe her perspective as 'systemic'. She encourages her coachees and clients to engage as many people as possible in the coaching process, and is a strong advocate of 'shadow coaching', a form of coaching in which she accompanies her coachees about the business, coaching them in the moment. Julie had read some adult development theory and recognises both her 'reactive self' and 'independent self'. She has received feedback on several occasions that she can come across as quite inflexible in the solutions she recommends. She would like to get to know her 'integrative self' better, and is looking for a supervisor able to articulate a narrative approach to working with adult development. Her specific focus on *perspective* is steering her towards a supervisor with whom she can engage in *reflective practice*, someone who she feels may already have a strong integrative coaching self.

Supervision as a means by which to have one's skills assessed, is very different to supervision as reflective practice. The coach interested in vertical development is only so likely to succeed without a reflective partner. To reflect alone often means going over the same ground again and again, through the same lens. A facilitated meaning-making process contributes to the acceleration of development.[9] If interested in vertical development, it may be important to choose a supervisor familiar with the concept. Such a supervisor is likely to understand the perils of constructing a development agenda built around a conscious intention to develop oneself 'vertically'. The supervisor is likely to encourage the coach to hold the model lightly, and stay focused on the needs of the client. The effective supervisor will be uncomfortable wearing the mantle of expert, and more comfortable playing the role of 'fellow traveller' or perhaps, at a push, 'advanced scout'. This is firmly the terrain of reflective practice, not evaluation and assessment.

There are many forms of supervision to explore: individual, peer and group supervision, for example. You may have a portfolio of needs and a portfolio of 'supervisors'. Whatever strategy you choose, we suggest you think about your development as a collective and ongoing journey.

Notes

1 Lots of stories. Send us an e-mail.
2 For example [Carroll, M. (1996). *Counselling Supervision: Theory, Skills and Practice*. London: Cassell], [Gray, D.E. (2007). Towards a systemic model of coaching supervision: Some lessons from psychotherapeutic and counselling models. *Australian Psychologist*, 42(4), 300–309] and [Gray, D.E. & Jackson, P. (2011). Coaching supervision in the historical context of psychotherapeutic and counselling models: A meta-model. In: Bachkirova, T., Jackson, P. & Clutterbuck, D. (Eds.) *Coaching and Mentoring Supervision Theory and Practice* (pp. 15–27). McGraw-Hill: Maidenhead].
3 Bachkirova, T., Jackson, P. & Clutterbuck, D. (2011). *Coaching and Mentoring Supervision Theory and Practice*. McGraw-Hill: Maidenhead.
4 Passmore, J. & McGoldrick, S. (2009). Super-vision, extra-vision or blind faith? A grounded theory study of the efficacy of coaching supervision. *International Coaching Psychology Review*, 4(2), 145–161.
5 For example, [Grant, A.M. (2012). Australian coaches' views on coaching supervision: A study with implications for Australian coach education training and practice. *International Journal of Evidence Based Coaching and Mentoring*, 10(2), 17–33].
6 Lawrence, P. (2014). What is coaching supervision and is it important? *Coaching: An International Journal of Theory, Research & Practice*, 7(1), 39–55.

7 Hawkins, P. & Smith, N. (2006). *Coaching, Mentoring and Organizational Consultation*. OUP: Maidenhead.
8 [Inskipp, F. and Proctor, B. (1993). *The Art, Craft and Tasks of Counselling Supervision. Part 1: Making the Most of Supervision*. Cascade: Twickenham] and [Inskipp, F., Proctor, B. (1995). *The Art, Craft and Tasks of Counselling Supervision. Part 2: Becoming a Supervisor*. Cascade: Twickenham].
9 Bachkirova, T. (2011). *Developmental Coaching. Working with the Self*. McGraw Hill: New York.

Last Thoughts

In this sort of book, it's customary to come up with conclusions. In the spirit of dialogue, however, we are interested in hearing what sense you made of this book, the conclusions you come up with. If you would like to share them with us we'd love to hear from you! Click on our website, look us up on LinkedIn, or send us an e-mail.

Paul & Allen
www.coaching3dimensions.com
paul@ccorgs.com.au
allenz_mail@yahoo.com

Index

action 14, 57
action modes 92–94
active listening 13, 21–22
adaptability 3, 51
affect 96
agility 112–113
ambiguity 1, 3, 47, 114
Ancona, Deborah 90
anxiety 14, 97
Association for Coaching (AC) 12–13
authenticity 130, 140

backward looking orientation 42, 58
Bowen, Murray 97
Bowen theory 97–99
Brock, Vikki 17n2

capability 7, 123–124, 129–132, 154, 157, 158
career planning 39
Cavanagh, M.J. 17n2
change 38, 120; change theory 15–16, 45–49, 107, 114; coach development 145–146; culture change 106–108; dialogic coaching 40, 41, 44, 56, 87; relational 126; resistance to 46, 47; systemic approach 56, 57; traditional approach 40, 56–57, 76
clarifying 90–91
closed systems 94–95

Clutterbuck, David 38, 89, 99–101, 120
co-creation 6; dialogic coaching 9, 24, 36, 42, 56, 57, 58, 85; goals 39; systemic coaching 58, 64; team coaching 90–91
coach, role of 42, 58
'coach validation protocol' 130–131
coaching: approaches to 2, 4, 5–6, 9–10; definitions of 110, 112, 117, 118; development 2, 4–5, 6–7, 123–124; practice 2, 4–5, 6, 61; see also dialogic coaching; systemic coaching; traditional coaching
'coaching cultures' 6, 107, 108, 109, 114–116
codes of ethics 13, 144
cognitive development 134
collaboration 77–79, 87, 109–110, 116
commissioning 90–92
communication 45–46, 96–97
competence 7, 41, 123–124, 125–128, 153–154, 157
competencies 14, 15, 57, 105, 126
complex adaptive systems 16
complexity 1, 76, 114, 133, 155; change theory 45, 47; competence 126; leadership 51; organisations 108; team dynamics 101

confidentiality 13, 15, 41, 42, 57, 58
conflict 83, 95
confrontation 65
Conklin, J. 51
connecting 90–92
constructive-developmental theory
    134–135, 151n4
consultation 46
context 33–34, 76–77, 78, 126–127
contracting 113
controlled discussion 25, 26–27, 32
conversations 24, 25, 27–30, 32;
    systemic approach 50, 56;
    three-way meetings 68–70, 72,
    73–74, 143
core learning 90–91
counselling 14
courteous compliance 93
culture 113; *see also* 'coaching
    cultures'; organisational culture
curiosity 3, 41, 52, 85, 147, 149

debate 24, 25, 26–27, 32
depression 14
development 2, 4–5, 6–7,
    123–124, 153–154, 155; case
    study 141–150; constructive-
    developmental theory 134–135,
    151n4; ladders 139–140; onion
    model 140; purpose of coaching
    109; stages of 133–134, 135,
    136–139; supervision 158–159;
    team coaching 89
dialogic coaching 5–6, 9–10,
    19–43, 44, 153; compared
    with other approaches 40–42,
    56–58; goal theory 37–40; group
    coaching 81, 82–83, 85–86, 87,
    105–106; identity 33–37, 42,
    59; managerial coaches 113;
    organisational coaching 105–106,
    111; team coaching 100
dialogue 5–6, 23–25, 30–33, 44, 57,
    63; change 40, 46, 49; feedback
    as 149; goal theory 37–40; group
    coaching 40–41, 81, 85; identity

33–37; multiple stakeholders
    76; organisational coaching 114,
    120; structural dynamics 92–93;
    systemic approach 9, 50–52, 53,
    56, 57, 78; team coaching 89, 99,
    100; three approaches compared
    58; three-coach approach 79
differentiation 97
divergent thinking 9
diversity 82–83
Drake, David 37, 41
duration of coaching 33
dyadic relationships 12–13, 41, 97

emotional support 156, 157
emotions 83
empathy 9
empowerment 117, 118
Erhard, Werner 17n2
European Mentoring and Coaching
    Council (EMCC) 12–13
evaluation 114–119, 120, 156, 157
evidence 125–126
experience 154
external focus 16

facilitation skills 80, 82, 87, 99–100
'facipulation' 46
feedback 70, 73–74, 75, 76–77; coach
    development 142, 149; evaluation
    of coaching programme 118;
    managerial coaches 112; from
    other coaches 132; purpose of
    coaching 110; 360 survey 72
'five disciplines' model 90–92
forward looking orientation 14, 42,
    57, 58
foundation skills 99–100
fusion 97

Gersick, Connie 89
goals: dialogic coaching 6, 22,
    37–40, 42, 57; group coaching
    81, 83–84; team coaching 90;
    three approaches compared 58;
    traditional coaching 13–14, 42, 70

Grant, A.M. 17n2, 17n7
group coaching 2, 6, 61, 80–87, 153; coaching the coach 86–87; dialogic coaching 40–41, 57, 105–106; difference between teams and groups 81–82; turn-taking 83–86; *see also* team coaching
GROW model 13–14, 38, 121n5, 144

Hackman, Richard 102n7
hall of mirrors 94
Hawkins, Peter 89, 90–91, 92, 111
hierarchy 20, 22, 45, 53, 117
holistic approach 6, 78; *see also* systemic coaching
horizontal development 123, 133

Ibarra, Herminia 37
iceberg metaphor 21
identity 52, 59, 130; dialogic coaching 22, 33–37, 42, 57, 59; three approaches compared 58; *see also* self
'imposter syndrome' 36–37
independent stage 137–138, 139–141, 143, 144–146, 150, 158
individual focus 15–16, 61, 63–79
influence 1, 11–12, 19–20, 22, 53, 65
innovation 51
integrative stage 138–141, 146–150, 158
International Coach Federation (ICF) 12–13, 14, 126
interpersonal coaching 78
Isaacs, William 24, 32

Kahane, Adam 23–24
Kantor, David 92–93
Katzenbach, J.R. 81, 102n7
Kegan, Robert 133–134
Kets de Vries, M.F.R. 103n12
'knowledge transfer' approach 107

ladders 139–140
leadership 2, 42; evaluation of coaching programme 115–116; feedback 77; leaders as coaches 111–113, 126–127; relational 15–16, 51, 58; systemic approach 50–52; three approaches compared 58
learning 7, 51, 82, 90–91, 99–101
Lewis, Laurie 46
listening: active 13, 21–22; coach development 148; controlled discussion 27; dialogic coaching 6, 21–22, 23, 24, 42, 56, 57; group coaching 84, 86; skilled conversation 29–30, 32; three approaches compared 58; traditional coaching 9, 40, 42; with or without parameters 25

managers: coach development 146, 147–148, 149; evaluation of coaching programme 116, 117; feedback 77; managerial coaches 111–113, 126–127; three-way meetings 68–70, 72, 73–74, 143; training 107–108, 111
'Manchester study' 15, 17n7
McCauley, Cynthia 151n4
meaning: coach development 143, 146, 149; communication domains 96; constructive-developmental theory 151n4; dialogic coaching 22, 40, 41, 57; perspective 123; social meaning making 49, 120; systemic leadership 51–52; three-coach approach 79
measurement 130–131
meetings: collaboration 79; three-way 68–70, 72, 73–74, 143
Megginson, D. 120
mental flexibility 130–131
mental models 59, 65, 132

monologue 23, 25, 29, 32, 46, 47, 49, 93
multigenerational transmission 98
multiple stakeholders 71–76, 78

objectives 111
onion model 140
open systems 94–95, 96
operating systems 94–95, 96
order 50
organisational culture 59, 96–97; culture change 106–108; purpose of coaching 110; team coaching 90; see also 'coaching cultures'
organisational development (OD) 15
organisations 6, 61, 78, 105–121; culture change 106–108; dialogue 114; evaluation 114–119; leaders as coaches 111–113; purpose 108–111
over-engineering 127

Parker, H.M. 17n2
partners 101, 158
Passmore, J. 17n2
patterns 53, 149, 153
perspective 7, 24, 70, 123–124, 133–152, 154, 157, 158
planning 45
plans 14, 22, 38
point-counterpoint 93
power 45, 47, 49, 53, 65–67, 96
process 88–90
professionalism 16, 41, 58, 59
punctuated equilibrium 89
purpose 108–111, 113, 115, 116, 117–118, 120

random systems 94–95, 96
reactive stage 136–137, 139–141, 142–143, 146, 150, 158
reflection 37–38, 75, 78, 131–132, 154

reflective practice 7, 147, 156, 157, 158, 159
relational leadership 15–16
relationships 2, 33–34; Bowen theory 97; change 47, 126; dyadic 12–13, 41, 97; interpersonal coaching 78; managerial coaches 112; patterns of 53, 153; systemic approach 6, 51, 65–67; team coaching 88, 89, 103n12
role identity 42, 58
Rommerts, Floris 32–33
Russo, Elaine 103n12

Schein, Edgar 103n12
self 36, 130, 154; Bowen theory 97; multiple selves 34, 41, 140; see also identity
self-awareness 6, 7, 83, 118, 131
self-criticism 65
self-development 130–131
self-reflection 130–132, 154; see also reflection
'shadow coaching' 158
sibling positions 98
skilled conversation 24, 25, 27–30, 32
skills: capability 7, 123–124, 129–132, 154, 157, 158; competence 7, 41, 123–124, 125–128, 153–154, 157; facilitation 80, 82, 87, 99–100; generic 107; managerial coaches 112, 127; measurement 130–131; supervision 158; traditional coaching 41; working with groups and teams 99–101
Slobodnik, A. 103n12
SMART goals 38
Smith, D.K. 81, 102n7
social-constructionism 33
Socratic listening 13, 29–30
solutions-focused approach 12, 14

stakeholder engagement 68, 71–76, 90
strategy 36, 111
structural dynamics 92–97
stuckness 93–94
supervision 7, 68, 131, 132, 147, 155–159
support 156, 157
system dynamics 99, 100
systematic perspective 50
systemic coaching 6, 9–10, 44–60, 153; change theory 45–49; collaboration 77–79; compared with other approaches 56–59; feedback 76–77; group coaching 81, 106; individual coaching 63–79; integrative approach 149; inviting the system into the room 64–76; leadership 50–52; managerial coaches 113; organisational coaching 106, 111; in practice 53–55; team coaching 89–90, 100

task, process as 88
team coaching 2, 6, 57, 61, 80–81, 88–101, 153; coaching skills 99–101; difference between teams and groups 81–82; 'five disciplines' model 90–92; managerial coaches 113; process 88–90; structural dynamics 92–97; team dynamics 88–89, 92–99, 100, 101; see also group coaching
thinking 7, 133
Thornton, Christine 88, 89, 99
three-coach approach 78–79
three-day intensive coaching 71–76

three-way meetings 68–70, 72, 73–74, 143
traditional coaching 2, 5, 9–10, 11–18, 52, 70, 153; compared with other approaches 40–42, 55–58; duration of coaching 33; group coaching 80–81, 82, 85–86, 87; managerial coaches 113; organisational coaching 105, 111; team coaching 100–101
training 107–108, 111
triangles 97
truth 24
Tuckman, Bruce 89
turn-taking 83–86

Uhl-Bien, M. 51
uncertainty 1, 3, 114
unconscious goals 39
unpredictability 47, 108, 149

values 78, 148; definition of coaching 110; 'five disciplines' model 90; self-reflection 130, 132, 154; stages of development 137, 138, 139
vertical development 7, 123, 133–140, 154, 155, 158–159
voicing 40, 56, 86
volatility 1, 47, 101, 108, 114

Wageman, R. 103n12
Watkins, Mary 140
Wheatley, Margaret 50–51
Whitmore, John 111, 121n5
Wilber, Ken 134
Wile, K. 103n12
work-life balance 26, 32